Just Between

Us Christians

Real Answers to Real Questions
Submitted by Real Christians

Dr. Lee Ann B. Marino, Ph.D., D.Min., D.D.

JUST BETWEEN US CHRISTIANS
Real Answers to Real Questions
Submitted by Real Christians

DR. LEE ANN B. MARINO, PH.D., D.MIN., D.D.

Published by:
Righteous Pen Publications
(An imprint of the Righteous Pen Publications Group)
www.righteouspenpublications.com

Unless otherwise noted, Scriptures taken from the Holy Bible, New International Version®, NIV®, Copyright © 1973, 1978, 1984, 2011 by Biblica, Inc. ™ Used by permission of Zondervan. All rights reserved worldwide.

Book classification: Books > Religion & Spirituality > Christian Books & Bibles > Christian Living

ISBN: 1940197562
13-Digit: 978-1-940197-56-2

Printed in the United States of America.

Ask and it will be given to you;
seek and you will find;
knock and the door will be opened to you.
For everyone who asks receives;
the one who seeks finds;
and to the one who knocks,
the door will be opened.
(Matthew 7:7-8)

TABLE OF CONTENTS

3   SORTING OUT OURSELVES   203

Word From the Author

Being a Christian isn't always easy. No matter what we do in this life, many desire we will fail. It's hard to make people happy, and even harder to live with the results of their displeasure. Many don't understand why we do what we do. Sometimes we don't even know why we do what we do. We fight misunderstandings about our beliefs, the negativity of those around us, our personal doubts about our faith, and do our best to persevere on, even when we don't understand where we are going or why God has placed us where He has.

That's where questions come in. In many Christian traditions, asking too many questions is seen as a negative. I believe the reason it is regarded as such is because people don't have the answers we need, so they try to dismiss questions as a lack of faith. This ignores the long, rich history we see in Scripture, especially when it pertains to wisdom literature. Books of Scripture – such as Job, for example – contain questions throughout. By asking questions, we get answers. By getting answers, we grow in our faith.

Yet many Christians fear judgment, alienation, and criticism for asking questions. We might find ourselves alone, without a safe space to help us sort out our thoughts and ideas. As a result, questions can go unanswered.

In this spirit, I welcome you to our safe place where no question is too big or too small, too insignificant or irrelevant, or too loaded to tackle. Whatever is on your mind is likely on the mind of another Christian who submitted a question, also seeking an answer. All questions are answered without judgment, criticism, or alienation to make sure we maintain the safe, secure place to discuss hard things. In these pages, it is my prayer that you will hear a true heart of honesty, Biblical insight, good humor, and even maybe an aspect of your faith, spirituality, or Scriptural knowledge that you never knew or considered before. It is all here, for the taking, ready and willing to transform your life, and push you to greater and more amazing things in Him.

No matter what you might have experienced in the past, know you have a home, here, ready to receive you, and to expound on anything you need to learn or explore, because here, even though we might not always get along, we are always family.

Dr. Lee Ann B. Marino, Apostle

SECTION 1:

SORTING OUT OUR FAITH

I pray that out of His glorious riches
He may strengthen you with power
through His Spirit in your inner being,
so that Christ may dwell in your hearts
through faith.
And I pray that you, being rooted and established
in love, may have power, together
with all the Lord's holy people,
to grasp how wide and long and high and deep
is the love of Christ, and to know this love
that surpasses knowledge—that you may be
filled to the measure of all the fullness of God.

(Ephesians 3:16-19)

How do I know I'm a Christian?

It's my personal belief that more question the veracity of their faith than they are willing to admit. We are afraid to admit it, fearing the criticism of others and confronting ourselves. It seems like a dark, deep, intimidating world to peer within, wondering what we will find as we take a journey into our own selves. How honest are we about what we believe? Do we really believe? What do we find within ourselves when the music stops, the lights go down, and it's literally just us…alone with God?

It's totally normal to ask this question and to ponder on it throughout your spiritual walk. It's not a sin, nor is it morally wrong. If anything, I think it's one of the most important questions we can ask. We can't reassess where we are at or examine our faith if we never ask the hard questions that bring us to a deeper place with God, and a greater realization of His place and presence in our lives.

The ultimate purpose of the Christian life is to know, love, serve, and worship God. How we do this varies a little within each believer, which can mean the way we express our faith is a little different in each person. It also varies greatly throughout the Christian walk, changing as time goes by. Within the framework of the Christian life are several different seasons, all with their own unique perspective. With those perspectives come different insights and different expressions of spirituality. It is for this reason the Old Testament School of the Prophets was over thirty years long; those who spoke for God had to understand how to hear from Him in good and bad times, with spiritual maturing, and through the challenges of everyday life. Even though we are not all prophets today, we can all benefit from this example, realizing that through our lives, the way we perceive our faith will definitely change.

The Bible tells us belief in Jesus Christ is central to our identity as Christians.

Then they asked Him, "What must we do to do the works God requires?"

Jesus answered, "The work of God is this: to believe in the One He has sent." (John 6:28-29)

What does "to believe" mean? According to the original Greek, the term "to believe' means "to have faith in or respect to; to entrust; to commit; to put trust with." In other words, God calls us to believe in Jesus – having faith in Him, committing our spiritual well-being to Him. This sounds great and good, but what does it mean in a practical, everyday sense? This sounds a lot like something we do one time and then we are good, so how does it work?

God doesn't promise us a rose garden for our belief; He promises us the assurance of eternity with Him. Between that point and our initial conversion, we experience many different things so we can learn to discover God's presence in our lives, even when things are difficult. This is not to say that everything that happens to us is "God's will" or that He "allows" things to happen like an evil overlord, but that no matter what happens in our lives, God is with us. It's the challenge of discerning that presence, no matter what – even in our darkest hours – that helps shape our belief in Jesus Christ. It is faith that endures; one that experience proves relevant and faithful and helps us see things from a spiritual perspective rather than a natural one.

Believing in Jesus doesn't fix all our problems, change all our circumstances, or even turn us into totally different people. We will still have interests and ideas that reflect our personalities. Our belief should help us improve our attitude, change our priorities, and transform by faith into better people, into individuals with a better sense of who God calls them to be and what God calls them to do. In the process, we learn more about God, love Him more, and also love others.

This process doesn't happen overnight, which is why I believe we get discouraged. Different issues come up repeatedly; cyclically, in fact, with new opportunities to address issues and see them from a different perspective. We grow; we heal; we change; we deal with new things. The cyclical nature of life makes us see how important our faith in Jesus is. As we believe and we grow closer to Him, we trust Him more.

I could provide a lot of theological jargon about believing in Jesus and what it means. Yes, we believe Jesus is Who He says He is; we believe in His divinity and His humanity; and while we don't fully understand this great mystery, we receive it by faith. Yes, we believe in what Jesus taught and fully seek to embrace it in a deeper way in our lives, which requires understanding and insight throughout our lifetimes. Yes, believing in Jesus means coming to know Him for ourselves. But ultimately, being a Christian – and knowing one is such – isn't so much about a doctrinal posture as living out our necessary spiritual cycles. If we are willing to stay the course – and apply what we believe – then we can know we are a Christian from season to season, in a way no one can take away from us.

I'M STRUGGLING WITH MY BELIEF IN GOD BECAUSE I HAVE TROUBLE UNDERSTANDING THE BIBLE. DO YOU HAVE ANY SUGGESTIONS?

I wish I could wave a magic "faith wand" for you and help eliminate your doubts, but I can't. Doubts about faith aren't as uncommon as many might like you to believe. I'd say it's probably safe to say most, if not all believers go through periods of questioning and doubt, sometimes more than once in their lives. All of us have questions about God, life, faith, the Bible, and the way these four often overlap aren't always clear or easily answered. When we go through periods of doubt, it is most important we press through them, seeking God and divine wisdom to find the answers we seek. We also need to seek out sincere and genuine support, rather than lip service, during these periods. It may mean finding new support or returning to places past, but it is important to know we have solid people in our lives to help through such inwardly difficult periods.

To specifically address why you are having doubts: the Bible is not a book that can be read like a novel, which I acknowledge you probably already know. Even though you know this, it's probably likely this has been your implied method of Bible reading. We don't often see the Bible approached through proper study and interpretation because much of Bible teaching skips over the full insight and context behind Biblical books and passages. It's hammered into our heads that if we have questions about our faith, we should read the Bible. This is great, but what happens when reading the Bible raises more questions about our faith...and we aren't given answers to our questions? What happens when we read those Bible passages where God seems cruel or inhumane? What about passages that seem to contradict each other? What about passages that leave huge, gaping questions in our understanding? What do we do when Bible reading opens the door for more questions, rather than less?

It helps to understand a few basic things about the Bible:

- The Bible is often thought of as being one "book," but it's a collection of several books authored over thousands of years. These "books" were originally scrolls or letters. In some instances, we know who authored them and at other times we do not. When they were first written, they were not divided up into chapters, headings, or verses. Sometimes there wasn't even a great deal of punctuation present. The current divisions, punctuations, and chapters we see in the Bible are there due to later translation and editing.

- Before the Bible was written down, its contents consisted of stories based in what is known as "oral tradition." This means these stories were told verbally, passed down between generations, in order to inspire and preserve faith. Sometimes there were thousands of years between the events that happened and the time they were written down.

- In between books, chapters, and sometimes verses there can be an unspecified duration of time. Between the book of Malachi and the book of Matthew, there is a four-hundred-year period of time. Unless such is specified, the Bible is seldom immediately chronological. There can be days, months, and even years between chapters, books, and some verses.

- The Bible is inspired ("God-breathed"), but that is different from thinking there is an "original" translation of the Bible or one that is more authoritative or infallible than another. Some people have translational preferences, but it is most important you find a translation you feel comfortable using and are able to understand. No Bible book was ushered down from heaven on a cloud. Inspiration teaches us that God has a hand in preserving, promising, and sending us valuable message and teaching through it.

- There are many different forms of writing present in the Bible: poetry, stories, histories, genealogies, songs, letters, visions, insights, sermons, and discussions. These different styles of writings provide different thoughts, feelings, and understandings of God, our relationship with God, and God's interactions with humanity.

- Different Christian groups acknowledge different books as having authority, or the more formal term, "canon" in the Bible. Some Bibles contain sixty-six books, some seventy-two, some more than that, and some less. Most books present in the western Protestant Bible are universally accepted, but there are some exceptions.

- The Bible was not written in English. Every translation we have of the Bible into modern language is a translation from its original Hebrew, Greek, and Aramaic tongues. The earliest translations of the Bible were in Syriac and Latin. In translation, some passages don't translate the same way as they did in their original language. Some don't translate clearly at all, and in some spots, we have no idea what the original authors intended to convey.

- The Bible itself is a record of God's interactions with those individuals He called to stand as His representative people throughout what we call "salvation history." It is not a record of every person's experience with God or even every person who was ever called by God. It's not a record of every single miracle, event, or incident God has ever done throughout history. In the Bible, we can see God's hand in creation from the very beginning, in calling people, in working in and through them, their successes and failings, and the formal establishment of a group by which His Son could come into the world. After Christ came, we find record of His ministry teachings, crucifixion, death, resurrection, and the community of believers who first followed Him. The Bible ends with pictures of what is to come, although we don't understand every detail or nuance of those images right now.

- Bible times were not like modern times. Bible times reflect totally different cultural traditions, ideas about governance and authority, societal custom, relationship dynamics, and priorities. The social and ethical mores of Biblical times were quite different than they are today. Some passages may seem extreme or hard to understand considering these differences. It doesn't mean we can't learn from these differences, but that we should familiarize ourselves with the details of these differences to gain a better understanding.

- The Bible's purpose wasn't to be the final answer to everything in existence. It wasn't penned, nor is it printed, to create conflicts between faith, science, medicine, and history. The Bible's purpose was to contain a faith record, to inspire on matters of faith, and show the ways human life overlaps with spiritual realities.

- When we read the Bible, we should see it living and relevant for us today. It shouldn't feel archaic but real, because it is about our faith experience as well as that of ancient people. Its inspiration makes us aware that it has the authority to guide and show us important things about our lives of faith.

- It is not possible for us to take every single passage of the Bible literally, in an application, all at the same time. To do so is both impossible and nonsensical. The Bible was not written all at one time, and it reflects culture, faith, social mores, and changing times. Our purpose is not to literally apply the Bible, but to see the record of what God has to say to us, right now, as we draw on the history and experiences of people in the pass. For Scripture to be fulfilled, we see it is lived, not static.

- Sometimes it probably seems like the Bible contradicts itself. It isn't that the Bible is contradictory, but different passages refer to different times and circumstances. Different circumstances sometimes require different actions, responses, or ideas. The Bible proves that our faith doesn't happen by itself, and God's leading or direction in a situation may vary, at times. It doesn't mean that truth is subjective, but that it is objective. It offers divine guidance, regardless of the situation.

I offer this information to you because we are often told certain things that can deter us from study and investigation when we don't understand something about the Scriptures. Contrary to what many say, you aren't going to figure everything out about God just from reading the Bible. It's a nice idea, but the Bible's purpose is a little different than some often make it out to be. When you read the Bible, you are reading experiences that individuals had with God, with themselves, and with others. It is a profound realization to see the Bible as experience rather than words on a page that we try to formulate into doctrine. I say this because when we understand it in this context, it becomes a lot more readable and understandable. It also helps us see God in an interpersonal way rather than in the sense of a dry doctrine. Just as much as God loved the people of old and interacted with them, so He does the same with you, too.

The Bible is supposed to teach us that faith enhances our lives and meets a deep need we have as people to experience the spiritual realm as we believe in God. By reading the Bible, we learn God isn't distant, far-off, or uncaring. If anything, we see just how much God loves His own despite their foolishness.

So how can you start to sort through the world of Scripture to understand this? I'd say the first thing to do is familiarize yourself with the Bible enough to know two key things:

- **Do you need a new translation?** – We tend to use the Bible translations that others around us use, not considering different translations serve different needs. The reason we have such a variety of translations is to help people with different levels of education, language skills, understanding, and spiritual call to understand the text in a way most befitting to them. There is no reason to use a Bible translation you don't understand.

- **Do you need a different Bible instructor or a different level of study?** – Sometimes Bible understanding gets lost in translation because we don't have the right instructors in our lives, those who can reach where we are at on our level of study. If you aren't finding a lot of insight or meaning into the Scriptures, it might be that those who are teaching you aren't relating to you in a way you can understand.

Where to start? The first thing I'd recommend is some prayer about these two starting points and direction therein. The second thing I would suggest is getting more familiar with the Bible. Daily or regular Bible reading can be a great place to start. Reading the Bible regularly familiarizes you with the people, places, characters, and contents. You to learn where books are located, where different Bible characters are featured, and have a better sense of what translations are best for your use.

I also encourage more in-depth Bible study for all Christians, especially in your situation. Learning about the people, places, culture, language, and life of those in Bible times helps us to better see through to what God said to them. This enables us to recognize what God has to say to us, today. Even though times and cultures have changed, we see human nature does not readily transform without divine intervention. We can also see God's constant love, no matter what culture or situation we find ourselves in.

There are a few ways to study the Bible. There isn't one way better than another, and most Christians will probably use a variety of these methods over time. There is hearing great preaching and teaching on the Scriptures, verse-by-verse study, chapter summary studies, book surveys, studying specific themes in Scripture, studying specific topics, and doing in-depth word studies. Exploring more of these different methods will help you gain better insight into what you seek out of Scripture and help you learn more in the process.

More than anything, I'd encourage you not to quit in your spiritual pursuits. The Bible is not here so we feel as if we can never question its contents or what is presented therein. Take the questions you have and use them to sort out your investigations, questions, ideas, and yes, even the points where you find yourself curious or dismayed. The Bible is a wonderful book with much to offer – take the plunge to dive in the right way and find yourself answers to every question you seek.

I'M UNCOMFORTABLE SEEING GOD AS A MAN. IS IT THEOLOGICALLY IMPROPER TO REFER TO GOD BY FEMALE TERMS, SUCH AS MOTHER?

We've all heard male pronouns applied to God. Whether it's Father, He, or Him, it can easily feel like God is a man in the same context of a man here on earth. This has led many to believe Christianity espouses a fully male view, one that does not include nor make room for anyone else.

In fact, when questions of feminine or neutral pronouns or entities for the divine arise, some protest the idea is blasphemy. Such is often labeled as part of a "feminist" or "queer" agenda. With threats like this, it sounds to some like pronoun usage should be avoided. This begs the question: is what they say true, and is it blasphemy?

I think we need to start by addressing that at the point of creation, God says the following:

Then God said, "Let us make mankind in Our image, in Our likeness, so that they may rule over the fish in the sea and the birds in the sky, over the livestock and all the wild animals, and over all the creatures that move along the ground."

So God created mankind in His own image,
in the image of God He created them;
male and female He created them.
(Genesis 1:26-27)

As one of the earliest passages in the Bible, God refers to Himself as "us." "Us" is decidedly not a male pronoun; in this particular instance, it is a neutral plural tense. If we understand the Godhead to have some sort of plurality to it (whether Trinitarian or Oneness), we recognize the fact that God is more than just one singular pronoun in personal usage. In Scripture, God has been revealed in plurality (such as Us or Them), as male (which is decidedly the strongest tone), and as female. Different terms are applied in different situations, depending on the narrator's tone and interpretation of the issues.

But beyond the issue of pronouns, we can identify something a bit deeper in this level of revelation. Being created "in the image and likeness of God" means we share in divine attributes by virtue of our creation. We reflect our Creator because we came from Him. We can think; to reason, to make decisions, and to reflect God's glory in our very being. What does this have to do with divine identity? Everything! God didn't just create "man," He created "mankind," or "humankind" in His image. It's not just men who are created in that image, but any being (women, nonbinaries, and agender individuals included) who classifies as being "human." We all have that divine stamp on our being, and that means all of us – no matter who or what we are – are just as much created in the image of God as another, regardless of how we might identify in gender.

This doesn't mean that God has "gender" in the sense that we often use the term. Human beings (people) are made in the image of God, but this does not mean God is a "person." Even though the use of the term "person" is of frequent use in early Christian doctrine, the use of the term "person" isn't used in the context we use it today. In ancient times, describing God as a "person" was reference to identity, personality, or animated being, rather than a literal human being. When the ancients attempted to describe God as a "person," it was to indicate God wasn't distant, far-off, or without a level of interest and animation we could relate to.

The complication with this human attempt to describe and define the divine has led many astray when it comes to how we understand God and our personal image of God. We think of God as a big version of us; looking like we do, without our limitations. This also means the exclusive use of such pronouns as He and Him makes people think that God is, above all things, just another man we must contend with and deal with in life.

This is not correct. The Scriptures tell us God is a spirit, and those who worship God are to do so in spirit and truth (John 4:24), not with gender or human labeling. When we come before God, we aren't coming before Him as a specified gender identity, but to worship Him in spirit and truth, receiving what He has for us as we offer all to Him. Gender is something that matters down here, not up there, which means it is not a part of entity, nor identity, in eternity.

When it comes to the struggle of divine identity, we still see the same issues today. Our language always limits ideas about the divine because language is something that identifies and describes what is down here. Nothing we can say can capture God in full, and that is true of our words, language, reference, and pronouns. The use of any pronoun, whether male, female, or gender-neutral does not come anywhere close to describing God properly.

In English and in many other languages, the use of male pronouns (He, Him) is inclusive of what we would call the "gender neutral" entity. It means people use such pronouns when they are not sure of gender and do such without deliberately excluding anyone else. Terms that are used in the Bible, such as "brothers" to describe the general body of believers, is an example of such. The limitations of human language make everyone "male" when in a group. It's limiting and a definite sign of patriarchy at work, but it also lets us know that when these things came up, non-male individuals knew they were not being deliberately excluded by writers. They were using the language they were familiar with, they knew they were part of things, and they accepted what was part of their world. This doesn't mean they never had their own thoughts or feelings, but it does mean they knew, as their language was written, they were still part of the church.

The ancients did not see God as being a limited male nor female. They viewed God as having the characteristics of both, all, and neither. This may sound complicated, and it indeed was. The ancient view of God was an evolving experience by which people knew and learned more about Him little by little. They didn't think they knew it all or had it all together, and they certainly didn't rest their assessments of God on human theological technicalities alone. They were people having an experience, and as they had their divine encounters, they learned more about divine attributes and aspects of God. They understood these attributes as either being identifiable on earth through male or female roles, at least in the most immediate sense. Those attributes that seemed to connect beyond this earth or transcend human experience were seen as being neither male nor female, but neutral in their application. The assignment of certain male, female, or nonbinary characteristics to God wasn't done to say God was a man, woman, or transgender individual, but to give illustration of those characteristics in a way that everyone could understand. The assignment of specified gender images is for our understanding – our benefit – but doesn't assign God a gender.

The Bible talks about God as Father; but it also talks about and describes God as Mother or in female terms:

As the eyes of slaves look to the hand of their master,
as the eyes of a female slave look to the hand of her mistress,
so our eyes look to the LORD our God,
till He shows us His mercy.
(Psalm 123:2)

But I have calmed and quieted myself,
I am like a weaned child with its mother;
like a weaned child I am content.
(Psalm 131:2)

For a long time I have kept silent,
I have been quiet and held myself back.
But now, like a woman in childbirth,
I cry out, I gasp and pant.
(Isaiah 42:14)

Can a mother forget the baby at her breast
and have no compassion on the child she has borne?
Though she may forget,
I will not forget you!
(Isaiah 49:15)

As a mother comforts her child,
so will I comfort you;
and you will be comforted over Jerusalem.
(Isaiah 66:13)

It was I who taught Ephraim to walk,
taking them by the arms;
but they did not realize

it was I Who healed them.
I led them with cords of human kindness,
*   with ties of love.*
To them I was like one who lifts
*   a little child to the cheek,*
*   and I bent down to feed them.*
(Hosea 11:3-4)

Like a bear robbed of her cubs,
*   I will attack them and rip them open;*
like a lion I will devour them —
*   a wild animal will tear them apart.*
(Hosea 13:8)

Jerusalem, Jerusalem, you who kill the prophets and stone those sent
to you, how often I have longed to gather your children together, as
a hen gathers her chicks under her wings, and you were not willing.
(Matthew 23:37)

Jerusalem, Jerusalem, you who kill the prophets and stone those sent
to you, how often I have longed to gather your children together, as
a hen gathers her chicks under her wings, and you were not willing.
(Luke 13:34)

The Bible describes God as giving birth:

You deserted the Rock, Who fathered you;
*   you forgot the God Who gave you birth.*
(Deuteronomy 32:18)

We also see God described as a woman looking for some lost money:

"Or suppose a woman has ten silver coins and loses one. Doesn't she light a lamp, sweep the house and search carefully until she finds it? And when she finds it, she calls her friends and neighbors together and says, 'Rejoice with me; I have found my lost coin.' In the same way, I tell you, there is rejoicing in the presence of the angels of God over one sinner who repents."
(Luke 15:8-10).

The Hebrew term for the Holy Spirit is feminine in form, not masculine. The Greek term in the New Testament is gender neutral but associated with female entity. The words for church, Scripture, love, and grace are all feminine in form. We almost never hear these facts, but they do prove God's identity in Scripture is not exclusively all one way or another. Embracing the fullness of God and God's nature is to embrace and understand every aspect of divine nature, despite the form it may take.

I would encourage you to embrace all that God is. This means if you can identify with God as Mother, then you are welcome to do so. God's point of identifying as Father or Mother is to embrace the role of God as a parent. If that's something lacking in your life, you can go to God, as His child, to embrace it. Start with what you can recognize, and come to see all of God, as God is, through your journey.

I DON'T UNDERSTAND WHAT IT MEANS TO HAVE FAITH AND HOW FAITH RELATES TO OBEDIENCE. CAN YOU EXPLAIN IT?

We've all heard emphatic messages from the pulpit, television, and social media saying we should have more faith. Often attached to such commands is the idea of obedience, especially "obeying God's Word." They are messages that are good at heart and sound real pious on the surface, but they often leave us hanging. When you start to get into life and faith in a deeper way, the question becomes, what does "having faith" mean? What is "obedience," especially "to the Word?" What word? And how do we figure out in any situation what such means?

Let's start by defining faith as is found in Scripture.

Now faith is confidence in what we hope for and assurance about what we do not see.
(Hebrews 11:1)

Hebrews 11:1 contains what is defined in theology and philosophy as an "ontological statement." This means it defines the nature of being and the properties and relationship between a thing and a subject. In plain English, Hebrews 11:1 defines faith for us by not just defining it, but by explaining the way we are able to identify it. Thus, there are two parts to Hebrews 11:1:

- Faith is the confidence, or in some translations, the "substance" of what we hope for. It is the content, the "stuff," of our hope, thus being in eternal or divine things.

- Faith is the assurance or reminder of those things that are eternal, which we cannot see. They are there to remind us of the things that we hope for.

Thus, Hebrews 11:1 teaches us faith is something that proves itself. It is both its own substance and essence. It provides us with hope and is the reminder of all we hope to see and achieve one day by itself.

We could say faith is an abstract concept made literal by our own practice. Whenever we stand on our faith, we are manifesting its promise in our lives. Faith, however, isn't something people can reach out and touch. It doesn't exist separately from our belief and our practice of it. There's no ghost outline of "faith" hovering around us. It is something we live by, something we believe in, and something we can't see without application.

That is where obedience enters the picture.

Hebrews 11:1 is the foundation to a long chapter that examines the actions of specific people throughout Old Testament history. As we read through the chapter, we learn the connection between their actions and their faith. They weren't people having random experience with random actions. They deliberately considered how their actions related to their faith and did what they knew was right within the realm of faith. This doesn't mean these people were perfect or did everything right all the time, but they saw the connection between their faith and their actions.

Where faith is abstract, the concept of obedience is not abstract. We are obedient to God when we make decisions and walk in actions that relate to and display our faith. Obedience is something we are taught, both by those who are here to help us learn and by divine experience. We come to learn what is best for us to do and what is most advantageous in the realm of faith as we walk with God and see how we can apply our faith to our different decisions.

When people talk about "obeying God's Word," they usually mean one of two things. The first is God's literal direction to you, given in some form. It might come in a prophetic word or a divine message, or it might just be what you know you are supposed to do in any given situation. The second is the advice to obey the Bible. This is something that sounds great as an advice, but as we've already explored in earlier questions featured in this book, obeying the Bible has an abstract quality to it, as well. We can't do everything that everyone was told to do, so it's better advice to seek the Scriptures for inspiration on how to better live your faith by looking at examples of obedience.

Discovering how to walk with God is a matter of allowing your faith to lead you in your life through steps of obedience. I believe people mean well when they make comments like we've discussed here, but I think in the long run they make it more difficult for us to sort out just what this stuff means for us. I'd encourage you to grow in your faith and learn more of just what you hope and believe in and then follow steps to bring those things to pass, one at a time.

Do We Have to Go to Church?

I once encountered a man online who discovered I was a minister. This led him to share all the issues he had with ministry, including the reason he didn't go to church: He was hurt at church a long time ago and hadn't returned since, having a real issue with church as a result. I retorted with the following evidence: He's surely been hurt at work, but he still goes there, he's gotten hurt at recreational events, but he still goes to those, he's had bad experiences at the store, but he continues to go there, and he has had bad meals at restaurants, but keeps going out. The defense that something happened at church and now he is totally opposed to going doesn't measure up. He didn't have a defense for my argument, and obviously, the conversation eventually broke down and went nowhere. I realized something important in this discussion for myself, though. No matter what people's justifications might be for not going to church, they don't go for one reason: they don't feel it offers them any personal benefit. If they believed going to church could benefit them, (much like other situations where things didn't work out like they liked) they would persist and find a way around them, anyhow.

Today's churches often market themselves in one of three different ways. We see churches that promote themselves as trendy and modern; ones that promote themselves as old-fashioned and in alignment with older ideas and concepts about church, and those that promote themselves as liberal and superior to other groups. While not all churches in existence fall into one of these three categories, these three are often the options that scream the loudest at potential churchgoers. As one assesses these categories, I feel it's a natural question to ask where one best fits and can get the most benefit.

I acknowledge the challenge involved in finding a church. It takes time and effort, which are sometimes things we would rather not do, especially when we have many other things to occupy our time. It is also sometimes difficult to know what one is looking for in a church, especially when every church claims to hold the answers. With Christian television shows bombarding the airwaves and numerous opinions about church online, what is the right way to approach church?

The first thing we need to clarify is yes, as a believer, you need to be in church. Your relationship with God is not just about you and Jesus. When you came to Christ, you were placed in His Body. God has done this for us not only for our support, but to force us to work out different issues within ourselves as we interact with others in community and family forum. If we disconnect from the church, it's easy to assume every idea we have, everything we think, and every belief we have is spiritually correct, when the opposite may be true. We are in church, in part, for the conflicts: for the situations that require reconciliation and forgiveness as much as those that don't, and to learn that our faith life is about our interactions with others as much as how we talk to God in our prayer closet.

Your church experience should involve worship of God, community involvement and development, learning about spiritual things that can be put into practice and applicable in your life, and provide a sense of belonging. It should also involve participation. We do not belong to church expecting to only get certain things out of it. We are there to give of our time, talent, and treasure as much as we are there to receive.

While you might not have all the answers upfront, it's important to know what these different things mean to you, especially in combination. That will help you best understand not only what you need, but where you belong.

Keep in mind: churches aren't perfect. They aren't supposed to be. It's in the imperfections of church that we grow and gain personal experience in applying the spiritual principles we learn therein. It's possible to attend a church with unreasonable expectations, thus rendering the entire experience null and void. No, not every church is for everyone…but that doesn't mean there isn't a church for you. Your church experience should challenge you, not agree with you about everything. That is, therein, where and how you grow.

There's nothing wrong with taking time to sort things out, but don't let that become a permanent state designed to keep you away from church. We all have bad experiences in many places, but that never stops us from seeing the value in the places themselves. The value we find in church is immeasurable, even if we must find a new one or a different one sometimes. None of us know it all no matter how close we might feel in our personal connection to God. We all need community to experience the fullness of spiritual life.

How do I discern my place in church?

Discerning what you are called to do and how you are best called to serve and fit within church is something that many dread. I'm not sure why this is. The discernment process to discover where you best fit in church is an exciting process of self-discovery. It helps you stand confident and assured in what God has for you to claim what God has for you in a new way, in a way that no one can take away from you.

The first thing you must do is remove any man-made ideas might have associated with the process. As we discover our placement, we often confront many concepts we often carry about ourselves, even unknowingly. If you have been in church for any period of time, you have already received a list of stated and implied rules about what is or is not deemed "acceptable" for you. These often vary by group, but they might be things about attire or physical appearance, personal conduct, relationships, habits, or political beliefs. Sometimes the things we are told are important – such as the things that relate to our faith and belief. This is not to minimize those, but to also state that sometimes we are indoctrinated into peripherals that don't really have much to do with our salvation versus things that matter. It's entirely possible for people to give us advice, believing they uphold something moral or purposeful, while misleading or hurting us. In this kind of state, we can be afraid to step out and try something new. Whatever regulations have placed on ourselves (no matter where they might originate) we have the challenge to remove those from our view. What God desires to do within us is whatever He desires to do, and we need to be open to discovery of that process.

As we come to discover our place within church, we may be confronted with where we are and what we need to do differently. We might have to find a new church, new leadership, maybe even new friends and a new attitude. We must get ourselves as right with God as possible to find our best place in church, and we need the right support to do that. If we are sincere and earnest, God will direct us we should be and connect us with the right people to help us discover our place in church.

The second thing you must do is approach your place in church with an open mind. There are many things we can do in church that aren't always obvious, and what God might have you do might not look like what someone else does. We are each a unique combination of spiritual gifts and abilities. Recognizing that the Spirit does a unique work within each of us can help you see just how special what you have to offer is for the church body.

The third thing I'd recommend is to try some different things that interest you. There are many ways you can volunteer, minister, serve, or involve yourself with a church community. Try some things out – some new and some where you expect to thrive. If you aren't sure where to start, pray and seek guidance from a trusted leader. You can also talk to trusted, spiritual friends who recognize and respect your desire to position yourself properly in church. These people should pray with you and encourage your direction, helping you to find something that will not just be best, but will be inspirational.

No matter your place in church, know you are called to participate, you are called to offer what God has given you, and you are always called to remain in the heart of God, developing greater relationship with Him. Finding your place may seem difficult but know that as you discern His voice and follow His will, you will always come out exactly where you should be.

What about those who've never heard the Gospel?

A fair question that many a Christian have pondered, it's obvious the top names in theology don't all agree on the answer. It's not uncommon to hear so-called experts claim those who have never heard about Christ or had the opportunity to be a Christian go to hell when they die. Some say those who haven't heard aren't accountable and therefore automatically saved, and others take a unique position, saying the people are judged as to whether they would believe if they heard. Who is right?

The simplest answer I have to this question is that the Bible doesn't clearly tell us what happens to those who've never had a chance to hear the Gospel, save what will happen to such individuals at the end of time (which I will speak about a little later). Based on what it does tell us about what is to come we can draw certain conclusions, but it still doesn't say outright what happens to those who have never heard.

The Bible is a record of a people who either heard and did better or heard and didn't do better. Its focus isn't on individuals who have never heard or had a chance to believe in Jesus, but of those who did have encounters with God and had a chance to do what was right in matters of their faith and their choices. It's as much about God reaching people where they are – in their mess, in their choices, in their mistakes, and yes, in their victories as well – as it is about people finding and discovering God for themselves. It's within these specific narratives that we discover what we might call the "tone" of the Bible. Even though some of its contents require more study and examination than others, the Bible's general purpose is to be a record of interaction: first with the specific group that encountered God first, and then the spread and inclusion of others throughout the known world at that time in history.

The question of what happens in the afterlife hasn't had a singular answer throughout salvation history. The earliest belief was the idea that everyone went to a singular resting place – the grave – while the spirit, or essence of a person, returned to its creator. As people grew in understanding of things such as moral conduct and spiritual purity, people began to differentiate between the wicked and righteous dead, with the option for the righteous dead to spend eternity in a place of comfort and safety, rather than torment or nothingness for the wicked. Throughout the years theological variants have emerged, often blending the idea of punishment for the wicked and paradise for the righteous in some form.

How one is determined "righteous" or "wicked" remains the multimillion-dollar question. How does one gain the magic entry into eternal paradise as opposed to an eternity of alienation or, more dramatic, torture? We can understand someone being sent to a place of punishment if they did something seriously wrong in this life, but what about those who never had the opportunity to decide for themselves if they were to be righteous or wicked? Are they held accountable in such a situation?

We know salvation is through Jesus Christ. As Scripture teaches us, there is no other Name under heaven by which people may be saved or spend their eternity with the Most High. For salvation to be possible, one must have some knowledge of Jesus Christ, understanding Him for themselves. It is in a much deeper context than just "hearing" something about Jesus and having a distant concept of Him as a historical figure; it is knowing and acknowledging His work for ourselves, and seeing that we can't do this life thing – whether now or forever – without Him. So, what happens to those throughout history who don't know about Him?

While it's probably safe to say we don't have a concrete answer, we can understand a few things based on our study of Scripture that can help us formulate a theory about what happens to those who have never had a chance to know of Jesus for themselves. The major passage that gives us the most insight is found in Revelation 20:11-15:

Then I saw a great white throne and Him Who was seated on it. The earth and the heavens fled from His presence, and there was no place for them. And I saw the dead, great and small, standing before the throne, and books were opened. Another book was opened, which is the book of life. The dead were judged according to what they had done as recorded in the books. The sea gave up the dead that were in it, and death and Hades gave up the dead that were in them, and each person was judged according to what they had done. Then death and Hades were thrown into the lake of fire. The lake of fire is the second death. Anyone whose name was not found written in the book of life was thrown into the lake of fire.

What we can know from this passage:

- At some point in the future, everyone will be resurrected. In the first verses of Revelation 20, we learn the saints, or believers in Christ, will be physically resurrected to rule and reign with Him first. We know from other passages that those who are absent in the body are present with the Lord, and therefore, they are with the Lord now in soul and spirit, awaiting this physical resurrection.

- Believers in Christ shall not experience the "second death," or eternal separation from God. Some call this hell, the lake of fire, or Gehenna. What exactly this experience will be like, we don't know. It is often depicted as torturous and fiery, but it's very possible such imagery exists to draw an illustration.

- Jesus shall sit on a great throne, somewhere within the realm and understanding of eternity. The unbelieving dead shall stand before the throne and shall be judged according to their deeds – what they did or did not do. How people will be judged or according to what standard is unknown, for good reason: such will be at the discretion of Christ, and given believers are not in the millennial judgment period, we don't know what "judgment" will look like.

- The mentioned "book of life" is known as the Book of the Dead in Judaism. It is considered a record of deeds one has done, especially those that are good or righteous, kind of analogous to a rollcall. In other words, the deeds of all are known before God, and those who are not part of the body of believers will stand present, with their rollcall examined.

- Death and the grave (hades) will be thrown into the lake of fire along with those judged wicked. Death will, therefore, no longer exist.

In connection with the question at hand, Scripture indicates everyone – including those who have never heard – will one day rise from the dead. Those who have not yet heard of it will face judgment for their deeds. This, therefore, offers both hope and information to those who have never heard the Gospel in their lifetimes.

WHAT DEVOTIONAL BOOKS DO YOU RECOMMEND?

Devotional reading is a beautiful part of the believer's life. I am a huge advocate of devotional reading because it is an intersection of both deep and practical spirituality. Our lives are often very busy, and it can be challenging to focus on long texts without distractions. We deal with the complications of work demands, church life, relationships and family, and sometimes the idea of reading a long chapter at some point in the day sounds a lot more like work than spiritual exercise. I have found devotional reading a great way to take that time and develop spiritual focus for my day, no matter how busy I might be. It resets with a short reading, doesn't take a lot of time, and gives much to think about as life takes its natural, daily course.

There are hundreds of devotional books in existence. Some I recommend:

- *God Calling* (A.J. Russell) – A.J. Russell is credited as author of this timeless work, but it was actually written by two women, known only as "the two witnesses." These short excerpts present themselves as a direct conversation with God, given in message form.

- *A First Book of Daily Readings from the Works of Martyn Lloyd Jones* (D. Martin Lloyd Jones as selected by Frank Cumbers) – A devotional book I could not put down, this compilation of excerpts from Martyn Lloyd Jones is theologically complex but simple enough that anyone can understand its contents.

- *Jesus Calling* series (Sarah Young) – A more modern approach to *God Calling*, *Jesus Calling* was authored by a woman who took the challenge to write down the words given to her in prayer by Christ Himself.

- *Let Go* (Francois de La Mothe-Fenelon) – A compilation of short letters written by a seventeenth century French archbishop and spiritual advisor that pack a strong spiritual punch when we seek inspiration and purpose in our everyday lives.

- *Madame Guyon's Spiritual Letters* (Jeanne Marie Guyon) – A collection of mostly short, easy-to-read letters from the 16th century prophetess, Madame Jeanne Marie Guyon.

- *Good Morning....God* (Pamela Steinke) – Written in a similar style to *God Calling* and *Jesus Calling*, this book inspires the reader to move from the anxieties of life into deeper communion with the Lord.

- *Spiritual Darkness Trilogy* (Lee Ann B. Marino) – Even though I am the author of this devotional series, I can attest writing all three of these books were a devotional challenge, in and of themselves. If you are in a place where you face spiritual darkness – whether through waiting, bitterness, healing, or the results of such times, this trilogy of twenty-eight-day devotional books is for you. Titles include *Waiting...Devotions for the Journey, Call Me Bitter: Devotions for the Hurting,* and *Healing Times: Devotions for New Seasons.* All three books are twenty-eight days in length.

There are also many books authored throughout the centuries that can prove useful and beneficial for devotional reading. As you take time to pause and read each day, it is my hope devotional reading will help you enhance your spiritual life, one paragraph at a time.

Do Christians have to Tithe?

Giving is a controversial subject in church. It almost feels like it is somewhat taboo; a topic to avoid only when necessary, and even then, it must be handled a certain way to render it effective. No matter how delicate an approach one might take with giving, someone is always going to be angry, disagreeable, or unhappy, without a doubt. Whether it's the question of giving financially, giving through time, or being generous as a person, it would appear the notion that Christians are called to give makes a lot of people uncomfortable.

Have you ever stopped to wonder what it is about giving that makes people uncomfortable? I believe there are a few reasons why it does, but perhaps the most relevant is because giving isn't meant to be fun. By its very nature, giving is meant to be sacrificial, meaning it costs us something if we do it right. When we give, we take part of what we have and offer it for the greater good of our Christian community. We give without condition, freely releasing what we have for the sake of spiritual benefit. It's good for us, it benefits the Kingdom of God, and it benefits others in the Kingdom. There's no way to lose with giving, and yet…we don't like doing it.

Ask people to do their best? They usually don't. Try to create some sort of exchange (such as offering volunteer time instead of giving money)? People still don't follow through. They will be quick to buy the latest gadget, fashion trend, or take an expensive vacation, but will claim they do not have money for giving. No one is going to tell them "what to do" with their money, even though advertisers and big corporations do it all the time and no one thinks about it.

Any moderate student of Scripture is probably aware that

giving is an essential part of Christian life. God gave Christ so we might live; for God so loved the world that He gave. He didn't keep the best part for Himself; rather, He gave of Himself. We learn about the essence of giving through God's example: If we love God, His work, and His people, we give. There's no other way around it.

For where your treasure is, there your heart will be also. (Matthew 6:21)

Each of you should give what you have decided in your heart to give, not reluctantly or under compulsion, for God loves a cheerful giver. (2 Corinthians 9:7)

It's clear the Bible tells us our priorities reveal a lot about us as people. Whether we are talking about finances, time, or use of our gifts, where we are willing to spend our money, time, and talents reveals what is most important to us. Such shows where our faith is at, how much we trust God, and how much of ourselves we are willing to give in His service. If we are willing to spend large amounts of money, time, and gifts on ourselves or other things but not on the Kingdom of God, that bespeaks a problem in one's faith.

The Bible addresses several different ways to give. All are required ways of giving for believers. These include giving of talent, time, and treasure.

- **Talent** – We are called to use the unique gifts and talents we have to build the Kingdom. The Bible itself does not indicate the number of talents and gifts matter, nor does it matter what they are. We have received them from God; thus we give them back in service to God. We should be active participants in church, offering what we have and discovering new things as we serve in church.

- **Time** – Every Christian should be volunteering in some way in their church. Most churches have several sub-ministries and subcommittees open to member participation. Whether it's nursery, Sunday School, audio/visual work, altar ministry, church cleanup, administrative assistance, or community outreach, churches need your time to expand the Kingdom's influence across cities and nations.

- **Treasure** – God also expects we give financially. Giving of our profit – whatever form that might take – is primary in the Kingdom, prevalent all the way back to Old Testament times. The most obvious way to do this is through a tithe: by donating 10% of your earnings to the church or ministry where you attend. Tithing was an ancient form of taxation, one that most notably kept the Levites (Old Testament priests) and temple operational from year to year. Tithing was not, however, where giving began or ended. Old Testament believers were also required to provide sacrificial offerings, offerings to support the poor and needy, and other gift offerings throughout the year. I once read that an observant Jew would have given away approximately one-third of his income.

When it comes to financial giving, I believe tithing is a good way to start. God gave us the ten percent income figure because if He left amounts up to humanity, they will give very little at all, if not nothing. It's a round figure, it's practical, it is easy to figure out, and it's something we all can afford to do. Being income-based, anyone can tithe, no matter how much or how little they might have. It creates a well-balanced situation where one recognizes church is not your only priority in life but is a priority. By setting aside that ten percent, one receives the benefit of commitment, the blessing of giving, and establishes themselves as part of God's kingdom – kind of like paying "Kingdom taxes."

I also believe giving to your church should reflect what you are getting out of your experience. Tithing is a great start and is often where people remain for several different reasons, but it's important to never forget we should give in other ways, as well. Sometimes a church has a special offering or project that needs financial support. Special events require additional funds as well as participatory support in the form of volunteers and time. If your church gives you the spiritual foundation you need, it should be your honor and privilege to support it.

So, to answer the question, yes, Christians should tithe. Tithing is giving, and God will never reject sincere giving. They should do much, much more than just tithing, however. Christians should give above their tithes as both required and necessary, be active participants in their community, and offer the gifts and talents God has given them for the spiritual edification of both themselves and others. Instead of worrying that giving costs more than we might like, we need to be open to give freely, without hesitation, and with cheerfulness. We don't give because we believe we are under a curse, but because we want to share from the bounty God has given us.

WHAT ARE THE GUIDELINES FOR FASTING WHEN MARRIED?

Fasting is one of those Biblical issues that comes up every so many years, often as a perceived "cure all" to anything and everything that seems to ail believers. If something seems amiss or problematic, it is often one of the first recommendations to solve the issue. Fasts are also called in ministries or churches for a variety of reasons: an upcoming special event, a pastoral change or departure, health reasons, or for decision-making. Fasting is used in different ways for different reasons; some are correct, some are not. To discuss fasting in marriage, I think we need to first understand what a "fast" is and how fasting applies in a marital context.

A fast is willingly giving up something to gain greater spiritual insight or revelation. It's not a diet or something done to lose weight or gain better health (although healthy weight loss is a great goal for one to seek outside of fasting). The purpose of a fast is to realize one's personal excesses and reduce or eliminate those excesses to see how they keep one from God or from spiritual insights, enlightenments, and goals. In properly understanding a fast to be a fast it must involve giving up one thing while practicing something else, such as prayer, devotion, Scripture study, charitable action, or some other practice that helps one gain spiritual focus.

Historically speaking, fasts have always involved food. People of old didn't have vast amounts of things to sacrifice in spiritual pursuit. Fasting from food was a huge deal. People in agrarian societies had to work hard physically, engaging in hours of physical activity and labor. Giving up food was the ultimate sacrifice many could offer, and it signified how seriously people took their responsibility to get right with God.

It was also common for those on a fast to abstain from all sexual activity. Sexual activity was seen an "energy drainer" and distraction when one wanted to get right with God. Abstaining from sex was seen as a spiritual discipline, controlling passions and desires, and gaining important ground in the development of self-discipline. If one couldn't be self-disciplined, it was assumed one would have trouble being spiritual.

As a result, when fasting in marriage is discussed, the major thing mentioned relates to sexual abstinence rather than food. 1 Corinthians 7:1-6 says:

Now for the matters you wrote about: "It is good for a man not to have sexual relations with a woman." But since sexual immorality is occurring, each man should have sexual relations with his own wife, and each woman with her own husband. The husband should fulfill his marital duty to his wife, and likewise the wife to her husband. The wife does not have authority over her own body but yields it to her husband. In the same way, the husband does not have authority over his own body but yields it to his wife. Do not deprive each other except perhaps by mutual consent and for a time, so that you may devote yourselves to prayer. Then come together again so that Satan will not tempt you because of your lack of self-control.

The contents of this passage have been discussed in many ways and interpreted in even more, but I think it is important to remember this passage is talking about sexual abstinence during a fast and when such is appropriate or inappropriate. There were people in the first century who believed any sort of sexual activity, in any context, was evil. They believed the material world was evil and anything that led to sensual or perceived pleasure was perceived as morally wrong. The Apostle Paul writes to correct this notion. Most likely as an asexual, he believed it was beneficial for people to be unmarried and celibate, because their attention was then undivided on the things of God. Even though his perspective might not have been considered the "norm," he acknowledges mandatory, long-term celibacy was unreasonable for most people. It wasn't practical to assume and perceive everyone could refrain from sexual activity throughout their lives. It was totally reasonable – and acceptable – for people to be married and desire a sexual relationship (if that is what both partners agree upon). But even in marriage, communication and respect had to be part of the sexual equation. Marital sexuality isn't a free-for-all, as some teach. Spouses still need to communicate with each other and recognize there will be periods of abstinence in a marriage, understood and discussed between spouses due to any number of factors: illness, post-childbirth healing, exhaustion, separation, physical incapability, or personal spiritual development, to name a few. Otherwise, spouses should consider one another's physical desires and needs and should be willing, eager, and even excited to explore the realm of their sexual relationship.

In considering one another's needs, when one is fasting – and sexual abstinence is involved – such should be communicated to and with a spouse. Couples should recognize and respect one another's decision to fast, through to the end. Such should be only for a period, as all fasts are done for only specified periods. All should be stated up front, clarified, and negotiated when necessary.

I do not believe a fast has to take one specific form, such as food or sex. I see value in both, but I do not believe those are the only two ways we can fast. The true purpose of a fast is to draw us closer to God, a fast should involve something that blocks or keeps us from God. We can fast from watching television or spending too much time on electronic devices or social media, spending too much money or over-spending on things we don't need, spending too many hours at work, distractions, bad habits (such as drinking too much coffee or soda or eating too much fast food or sugar), destructive relationships or behaviors, or from any other thing that dominates our lives and blocks our spiritual insight. If we start to see fasting like this, we should take time to select something keeps us from God because the associated behaviors can be destructive to our spiritual lives.

No matter how we desire to fast I think it's a great idea to discuss it with your spouse. The Apostle Paul encouraged such conversation and mutual decision to encourage communication about things in life that might keep you away from God. Behind every fast is a desire to draw closer to Him. Any spouse who truly loves you will encourage you to delve further into your spiritual pursuits. A good conversation about a fast also has the power to influence your spouse to recognize areas of their life that also need discipline and spiritual insight. Such can work powerfully to bring the two of you together, as well as draw the two of you closer to where you desire to be with God.

In this, we learn the communication of fasting. Our desire to withdraw and remove something from our lives is a message we send to God, ourselves, and those around us. If we view fasting in this light, it should help us to articulate our spiritual interests and desires, especially with those closest to us. We learn to balance these desires with the cares of life. By doing so, we find God in our seeking, through things ordinary and most sacred, and even in the intimacy of married life.

Head Coverings in Church – Yes or No?

Ah, head coverings. This is one of those topics some people approach with total ire, and others with total revulsion. It isn't an issue we see much anymore unless one is a member of a denomination that requires it. It's been a long time since I've been asked about this issue, but I am glad it has come up, nonetheless. I think the heading itself – and what is addressed alongside it in Scripture – merits a conversation, especially as applies to women.

The Biblical injunction about women and head coverings comes from 1 Corinthians 11:2-16:

I praise you for remembering me in everything and for holding to the traditions just as I passed them on to you. But I want you to realize that the head of every man is Christ, and the head of the woman is man, and the head of Christ is God. Every man who prays or prophesies with his head covered dishonors his head. But every woman who prays or prophesies with her head uncovered dishonors her head—it is the same as having her head shaved. For if a woman does not cover her head, she might as well have her hair cut off; but if it is a disgrace for a woman to have her hair cut off or her head shaved, then she should cover her head.

A man ought not to cover his head, since he is the image and glory of God; but woman is the glory of man. For man did not come from woman, but woman from man; neither was man created for woman, but woman for man. It is for this reason that a woman ought to have authority over her own head, because of the angels. Nevertheless, in the Lord woman is not independent of man, nor is man independent of woman. For as woman came from man, so also man is born of woman. But everything comes from God.

Judge for yourselves: Is it proper for a woman to pray to God with her head uncovered? Does not the very nature of things teach you that if a man has long hair, it is a disgrace to him, but that if a woman has long hair, it is her glory? For long hair is given to her as a covering. If anyone wants to be contentious about this, we have no other practice—nor do the churches of God.

This is a very complex passage for interpretation. The entirety of the section doesn't make a lot of sense to our modern-day sensibilities. I might even say it is a bit confusing because there are multiple references to different cultural and traditional ideals. There are a couple of things that are obvious, but we often miss them in the language of the passage. Let's start with what we do – and can – clearly recognize.

The first thing: the passage is talking about women who pray or prophesy, just as it speaks of men who pray or prophesy. In other words, the discourse is about public prayer or public speaking, not private prayer. This means the injunction for women being "silent" in church found later in 1 Corinthians 14 wasn't an injunction against women in ministry. It also was not to be a permanent state for church women for all time. When examining that passage, we must consider the context of this one, as well. There must have been specific situations or issues present in the Corinthian church to raise these issues without contradiction. (I will discuss what those were after we discuss more of what is obvious here, in this passage.)

The second thing: It is obvious the Apostle Paul cared enough about the women of Corinth to see they were not doing things perceived as dishonorable or disrespectful in some form. Whether or not we always recognize it, the Apostle Paul was interested in female participation within the church. It wasn't his hope or desire for women to be downgraded or ignored in church. He believed they should be taught about things they never had the chance to learn about prior. When it came to presentation and conduct, women needed to learn what to do (just like others did) and they needed to have the opportunity to exercise their spiritual gifts and abilities within spiritual decency and order.

The third thing: All in the body of Christ (whether male, female, or nonbinary) are interdependent on one another in spiritual assembly, not independent of one another. What this means is all of us, no matter our gender, are needed in church. This passage, nor any others of the Apostle Paul, were meant to exclude anyone from assembly participation. We all have gifts, and those gifts require we offer them for the greater good of the church. The interdependence of humanity is displayed in the specified creation of male and female, which is shown by origination: woman as taken from man, and all being created for an eternal purpose.

Now that we have discussed the obvious things, let's look a little more carefully at the issues and culture present which impact on the way we are able to understand this letter. Corinth was an ancient Greek city, known for its strong pagan culture. The church was trying to find a way to not only survive but grow within a society that was antithetical to everything Christian. The mixture of Greeks, Romans, Jews, pagans, and other cultural and spiritual converts led to conflicts and confusion over what was allowed, disallowed, or permitted therein. There were many questions, curiosities, and yes, mishaps as the church tried to find its footing.

As a church with many pagan converts, the church faced

the inevitable "mixing" of doctrine and practice. When such arose, the issues at hand needed to be addressed. Yet the Apostle Paul also strove for the Corinthian church to fit in with their culture and times, because such would provide a more effective witness than dressing, eating, and engaging different from others around them.

The Apostle Paul's advice about head coverings for women was issued to the Corinthians as a statement of culture: they should follow the fashion trends and local customs present in Corinth at that time. To present themselves in public unveiled would have caused the women to be viewed with suspicion, immodesty, or disrepute. Such appears to have been especially true if it was done by a married woman, because doing so would bring repute not just to herself, but also to her husband. By quoting the Talmud (where he speaks of a woman's head covering due to angels), he is affirming this custom of public head covering is not in conflict with any spiritual tradition, neither Jewish nor pagan. To follow such was appropriate within Corinthian culture for women who speak and present themselves in public worship. Head coverings were a sign of authority and a woman taking such authority, rather than a sign of degradation or humiliation.

This doesn't mean that women would have to cover their heads in every assembly worldwide, even in the first century. The Apostle Paul affirmed their cultural dress was in no way inappropriate, nor a threat to the Gospel. It was perfectly fine to dress with the times and follow custom, no matter where they were. Not being about the physical garment (a veil, a hat, etc.) the idea was more relevant – and focused – on cultural adaptability and the ability to maintain cultural dress and practice in church, no matter where we may be.

For example: In Genesis 38 we see Tamar veiling herself to

work as a prostitute. Such was a visible sign, a connection, to the life of prostitution in very ancient times. In Corinthian culture, veiling oneself was seen as a sign of self-respect and cultural authority. Times change, styles change, association with specific garments change, and cultural trends change. The Apostle Paul gives us the foresight and acceptance of such, without reservation.

The same is true with other issues addressed herein, such as the length of a man's or woman's hair. We don't have a definition for just what is "long" or "short" in this passage. There's no specific length a woman's hair must be, or a man's hair cannot be. In some cultures, women have short hair. In some, men have longer hair. Cancer treatments or some illnesses cause hair loss, which can be permanent. Some people just don't have a lot of hair. Some hair types don't grow long by natural means. No one is prohibited from church leadership, prophetic word, or engagement based on the length or amount of hair they have. The passage is an emphasis on cultural adaptation, feeling free and engaged to interact with those in one's culture, whatever and wherever it might be.

To answer the question for modern times: women are not required to wear a head covering for spiritual purposes or as some sort of sign of male dominance; they never were. If a woman is in a culture that does not require head covering as general social practice, it should be the woman's choice to wear a hat or a veil for fashion purposes only. It is perfectly acceptable to wear a head covering or not wear one in such circumstances. If a woman is in a culture that embodies head coverings as part of general life society (she would wear one anywhere she goes), then head covering is part of her culture. She should not feel forced to remove such to make a specified point. The use of a head covering is a cultural one, not a religious practice. Both are fine and understood to be reflections of where a woman lives, and what is associated with such, rather than a mandate for spiritual living or theological practice.

CAN WOMEN SPEAK IN CHURCH?

As a woman in ministry, I've been asked this question more times than I care to remember. It is based on what I call a "clobber passage," because it is only used with one intention: to shut down anyone who might do something that appears (hence appears) in contradiction to it. Clobber passages aren't used to defend solid theology. They are used as weapons to create blocks and problems for people in Bible understanding. In the long-term, these verses are deliberately positioned to cause hurt and offense.

The "clobber passage" in question is found in 1 Corinthians 14:34-35:

Women should remain silent in the churches. They are not allowed to speak, but must be in submission, as the law says. If they want to inquire about something, they should ask their own husbands at home; for it is disgraceful for a woman to speak in the church.

Given what I addressed in an earlier question (*Head coverings in church – yes or no?*), how do we address this passage in a complete picture of Scripture? How do we understand it?

1 Corinthians 14 is a long chapter that addresses issues of order in worship. As I stated earlier, Corinth was a pagan city. The Corinthian church had several pagan converts; some strove to overcome their pagan ways, and others weren't quite so ambitious. Being they existed in a pagan community, they were not familiar with traditional Jewish order or structure present in synagogues. Men and women had different roles within pagan communities than they did in Jewish custom. Women were in no way part of the public life

of Jewish worship. They were not taught, learned, or educated in the faith. What they knew of Jewish custom came through association: overheard or active conversations with their fathers or husbands, sacrificial offerings or standing on the fringe of ceremonies, or through the words of prophets. In pagan custom, women fulfilled the role of temple prostitutes and oracles, and were, by nature of magic and certain rites, an active part of their community. They would have had no knowledge, nor understanding, of salvation history. Bringing the two groups together, complete everyone having different backgrounds, roles, and understandings would have rendered a crazy, messy assembly.

The Apostle Paul wrote about order in worship to this church because it clearly lacked it. He didn't just address one issue, but many: how to handle public gifts (such as speaking in tongues), giving a word of instruction, and prophecy; the importance of providing proper edification in the church; order of service; and, above all, how all these things lead to the education of the church. This is where 1 Corinthians 14:34-35 comes in.

The early church didn't have "new believer" classes or Sunday School programs like we have them today. Often, they had a private teacher who worked with new converts, seeing the believer from initial desire to believe through to baptism and beyond. Whether or not this practice existed among women in Corinth is uncertain, especially considering the issues present in this passage. It is obvious women did teach and assist other women in congregations, but it is very possible the church at Corinth wasn't even this structured. The first-century churches weren't a consistent bunch. Programs and ideas evolved as necessary, and you weren't guaranteed to find the same exact program in every place. From what Corinth sounds like, female converts were thrown into the mix along with everyone else, with little background instruction. Whether their husbands were Jewish or Christian, they probably wouldn't have thought to try and teach their wives at home. This means the women continued to miss necessary education and discourse, including salvation history. No matter how you want to spin it, the women were playing an endless game of catch-up.

These facts are necessary to understand the situation the women of Corinth faced every time they gathered to hear a message at church. The passage in question doesn't speak about all women; it specifically addresses wives. In ancient assemblies, women and men were often separated. The women sat in one place, and the men in another. From what we know of Corinth, if the women had questions about what was going on, they were quick to disrupt the meeting by asking their husbands on the other side of the room, hoping they would explain what was being said. If the men were to respond, they would call back and forth to the complete disruption of the meeting. Chaos could easily ensue, not to mention the focus of the meeting was entirely lost. These women weren't seeking out the speaker for advice but their spouses, and that meant they would distract from the speaker's words as they shouted back and forth with their husbands.

The married women of Corinth were learning the great message of salvation for the first time. They were also drawing on their chaotic pagan background, as temple rites weren't as structured and ordered as Christian services. Acting disruptive wasn't as notable in a pagan environment, so these women thought nothing of asking something any time they felt like it. They were also used to having a certain level of power, as pagan fertility rites couldn't happen without them. To them, they had no idea what was going on and had no problem trying to find out, even if such was disruptive.

Recognizing the situation, the Apostle Paul mandates these women should attend service and listen – rather than speak – submitting themselves to the order of the service. They were learning, so they should be silent. If they had questions, the public assembly was not the time to ask their spouses. Instead, they should have discussion and instruction with their spouses at home, where they could receive one-on-one attention and interest in their specific questions rather than disrupting the meeting.

It's not that all women speaking in church was disgraceful; it was the type of speech, rooted in the way these women were conducting themselves. It's obvious not everything a woman had to say in church was disgraceful, because a few chapters over, we learn about women praying and prophesying publicly. The issue wasn't being female, so much as addressing an issue that was prevalent in women in Corinth and has now been preserved for our instruction while learning, even today.

I think we need to realize we often take gender-specified passages very personally, and for good reasons. It seems as if the church world takes great pleasure in treating women differently than men. But why does this passage have to be understood to just be about women? It extends to anyone – and everyone – of any gender – who is learning about Christian doctrine and protocol for the first time. We should all learn quietly, listening and paying attention to what is said. Such shows respect for the speaker as well as for God. It also ensures we won't miss anything due to lack of attention. When we are in a public assembly, we should all follow the rule of being attentive and quiet. We should also expect those around us to refrain from becoming a distraction.

I am not opposed to ministers holding question-and-answer discussions after messages, but I also acknowledge such is not always possible. If you have questions after a service, I think it's great to make contact with the speaker to discuss whatever is on your mind more in-depth at a later time. If you have a spouse, home discussions about things of faith can be a great way to connect the two of you in a deeper sense. Small group Bible studies are also a great solution for greater learning. These avoid public disruption and help keep group events focused.

1 Corinthians 14:34-35 wasn't meant to put women "in a place." It was meant to help edify them in their faith, to give them the necessary footing to learn, and to reach a mature stature in the faith. It was never about women not teaching or never speaking in church, and it was certainly not put there to clobber women who are in ministry. It was a step up for women, giving them their first-ever opportunity to hear about salvation and grow in Christ.

WHAT DO YOU SAY ABOUT SUBMISSION?

Submission is a word that most people cringe when it comes up. This is especially true for women in church, as we do so by association. All of us, in some form or another, have had it hammered into our heads that we can't do this or that because of "submission." Whether it's because of submission to a leader or submission to a man, many avoid the topic all together. We are afraid of submission; we think it means we are less than someone else, and we are often told that's exactly what it means. Submission is taught to be degrading, a sign of being second best and of lesser importance than someone else.

Submission is a principle of life and living. It doesn't mean, nor indicate everything we've been taught about it. It is something every person on this earth, whether male or female, must do at some point in time. Understanding this and embracing it is one of the most important things we can ever do. If we don't do it, we will find ourselves in situations that cause heartache and personal loss, and ultimately, we may lose our lives.

I mention this because every one of us "submits" in some way to someone else, every single day. We submit ourselves:

- When we are at work on time.
- When we complete our required tasks as part of our job requirements.
- When we are part of a church and we acknowledge the leadership therein as our personal spiritual leadership.
- For church service, when we are punctual and properly involved.

- Whenever we pray, praise, or worship God.
- When we refrain from arguing about something that is simply not worth arguing about.
- When we pay taxes and follow specified government regulations or laws.
- When we follow given instructions in a situation or directions to accomplish or complete a task.
- When we do or offer something for someone that they will like or enjoy.
- When we relinquish our way about a matter.
- When we admit we were wrong about something.
- When we encourage someone else to do their very best.
- When we humble ourselves in any given situation.
- When we agree to follow and obey the will of God.
- When we do something we don't want to do, but know it is the right thing to do.

It's evident from this list that submission isn't something foreign. We might not consider what we do in these situations to be "submissive," but that is exactly what they are. Sometimes it is easier to accomplish than others, but somewhere inside, each one of us recognizes submission can be of benefit. Submission's catch is that we often use it for manipulative ends. It is easy for us to walk in a submissive spirit when we want something from someone or desire to gain something from God. We find it within ourselves to do our best possible job or follow the necessary steps to get a promotion, often with excitement and anticipation. We find it easy to apologize if there is some obvious benefit in doing so. We will hold our tongue if doing so assures us we get whatever we want in a situation. We know how to be submissive when it is beneficial, but when it doesn't seem to be of any obvious benefit, it's something we suddenly don't want to do.

I make this point for one simple reason: we understand submission as a general principle. We understand humbling ourselves, refraining from esteeming ourselves more highly than we ought, sticking things out, following rules, and participating in things is to our benefit. We get all these things in a general sense. But when we start talking about submission, we all get angry, uncomfortable, and feel degraded.

We feel that way because that's how people make submission sound. They talk about it, rather than as a principle, as something to put us in a certain "place." We can be in situations where we submit all day long, but if we start attaching more to it, it is then used as a means of oppression. This is an example of the way that basic life – and spiritual – principles can be easily distorted into something else.

Submission is, in essence, the ability to humble oneself before another. In submission, we don't esteem ourselves more highly than we should. This doesn't mean we debase ourselves or that we are nothing, but we acknowledge that others in our lives have certain positions or authority, and we respect those. We also honor and respect relationships in submission when we are willing to admit we have been wrong or value a relationship more than we value getting our way or trying to be right. That is what makes submission a spiritual principle; it is something we do because we know it is right.

When it comes to our personal relationships, I ascribe to the belief that submission is mutual, and not exclusive. When submission is not mutual, situations quickly become abusive. I do not believe having to humble oneself only goes one way in a relationship. I also do not believe God intended to give such a message about personal relationships. We will forever have gifts, talents, abilities, and spiritual priorities that will cause a mutual dance of submission: where both parties submit themselves to God's will and in action, to the needs and priorities both have in any given situation. It is an art form as we learn how to esteem each other, respect one another, and encourage one another to be all God has for us to be, one situation and circumstance, at a time.

Submission is also a powerful place of trust in any relationship, especially in our relationship with God. We should trust those we know intimately. The situations we find therein should not demand our need to assert personage all the time, because such should be acknowledged and respected. If you are in a relationship where you do not know and do not feel assured someone seeks your best and desires you to find and have all God desires for you, you are in the wrong relationship. No relationship is powerful enough or great enough to ever convince us we aren't enough, and if we find ourselves fighting, that's a pretty good indication the relationship is not one where you find yourself able to grow through your relationship dynamics.

If we must maintain permanent control of everything all the time, there is no time to develop the attributes and insights God seeks to bring to us. We must trust those with whom we are intimately involved unto the end of knowing what's worth pursuing and what isn't. It also helps us to work out our own character flaws and issues, things that keep us from advancing; as we learn when to fight, when to let go, when to seek God, and always, when to grow.

As I showed in the examples above, people of every gender practice submission in different situations. It's not exclusive to any one specific group of people. In fact, if we look at the Scriptures, our ultimate lesson and understanding is to stand before God in submission. As we learn to obey God, we find ourselves humbling ourselves rather than demanding our way. Submission is something we all do and are called to do; it's for all of us. The sooner we learn to seek it out in our own unique way, for our own calling, the better we will be.

WHAT IS "MODESTY?"

If you've spent any time in church, you have probably noticed an abnormal amount of attention paid to women's attire. Even though ideas about modesty did extend to men at one time and still do in some groups, modesty is definitely one of those issues that seems dumped on women. You have probably even experienced the sting of judgment when it comes to the ire of someone who just doesn't think what someone else is wearing measures up. It seems like no matter what someone's wearing, someone else has a problem with it. We are unsympathetic to wardrobe mishaps or accidents when clothing just doesn't do what we anticipate it to do, thus causing a lot of women to spend time worried about their clothes, whether such is necessary. To make matters worse, it's all done in the name of "modesty," which we are always told is a Biblical virtue.

Just what is "modesty," and how does it relate to our clothing?

Surprise: Biblical modesty is always in relation to money, not the sexuality or attractiveness of attire. Whenever the Bible talks about modest attire, it is speaking about women (men are also included but women are often mentioned) who desired to stand as "society" women and flaunt their wealth and social status above others, even in church. This was done through elaborate hairstyles, jewelry, and specialty fabrics and colors in their garments. Without speaking a word, they sent others a message of societal superiority. Such couldn't be tolerated in church, as it would destroy the unity and very message of spiritual equality present therein...thus the issue had to be addressed. Those who were flaunting their wealth through their clothing needed to tone it down. This would help others to feel more welcome and involved as part of spiritual assemblies.

There's nothing wrong with wearing your mother's pearls (or in my case, my long fake set), your grandmother's earrings, or looking nice or fashionable in church. The purpose behind Biblically modesty was to avoid a negative social statement, not one that says you're interested in fashion or presenting well before God and the church. It's fine to have interests, it's fine to desire to look nice, and it's fine to stand before God and others properly dressed – it's just not fine to do it to show up everyone else in the room. God calls to mind our motives rather than the actual garments we may wear, no matter what the circumstance may be.

Thus, dressing modestly isn't about sex or sexuality in the Bible. However…this does not mean we shouldn't use good judgment in planning our attire or how we choose to present ourselves when in God's house. Our attire should not serve as a distraction from the purpose and heart of why we assemble in church: to worship God. We should never deliberately wear clothing that is too tight or too short in church, because such things can prove to be distracting (not just to others, but to us as well, because it can be uncomfortable). This doesn't mean we have to dress in sackcloth and ashes, either. Finding a good middle ground is a thing, and an important part of moderation with any issue we might face. We can dress respectably without wearing a skirt all the way down to the floor. It's important to teach everyone in church – male, female, and non-binary – about proper attire that doesn't distract as we come to worship God. As a general rule for all people who attend or serve at church, it is essential to wear clothing that fits properly, that is comfortable while one wears it, and that helps us look the part while keeping our focus on God and spiritual things while in worship services.

Is Submission Required for Wives?

The best place to start with marital submission is to understand where the concept comes from and why it's included in Biblical text. From this, we can better understand what God teaches us. Even though you would be correct in stating the way it is approached is very outdated, the lessons that God presents about Christ and the church are worth a second glance, especially in the context of their purpose in marriage.

What is commonly known as the "doctrine of submission" is found exclusively in the New Testament:

Submit to one another out of reverence for Christ.

Wives, submit yourselves to your own husbands as you do to the Lord. For the husband is the head of the wife as Christ is the head of the church, His body, of which He is the Savior. Now as the church submits to Christ, so also wives should submit to their husbands in everything.

Husbands, love your wives, just as Christ loved the church and gave Himself up for her to make her holy, cleansing her by the washing with water through the word, and to present her to Himself as a radiant church, without stain or wrinkle or any other blemish, but holy and blameless. In this same way, husbands ought to love their wives as their own bodies. He who loves his wife loves himself. After all, no one ever hated their own body, but they feed and care for their body, just as Christ does the church — for we are members of His body. "For this reason a man will leave his father and mother and be united to his wife, and the two will become one flesh." This is a

profound mystery—but I am talking about Christ and the church. However, each one of you also must love his wife as he loves himself, and the wife must respect her husband.
(Ephesians 5:21-33)

Wives, submit yourselves to your husbands, as is fitting in the Lord.

Husbands, love your wives and do not be harsh with them.
(Colossians 3:18-19)

Wives, in the same way submit yourselves to your own husbands so that, if any of them do not believe the word, they may be won over without words by the behavior of their wives, when they see the purity and reverence of your lives. Your beauty should not come from outward adornment, such as elaborate hairstyles and the wearing of gold jewelry or fine clothes. Rather, it should be that of your inner self, the unfading beauty of a gentle and quiet spirit, which is of great worth in God's sight. For this is the way the holy women of the past who put their hope in God used to adorn themselves. They submitted themselves to their own husbands, like Sarah, who obeyed Abraham and called him her lord. You are her daughters if you do what is right and do not give way to fear.
(1 Peter 3:1-6)

As I already addressed in an earlier question, (*What do you say about submission?*) submission is not a principle quite as foreign to us as we might like to think. It is also not something exclusive to any one gender, as it's not practiced by only one gender. So why the specific injunction about submission for wives?

To many, especially those who study the Scriptures in-depth, these passages may seem odd and out of place. Both the Apostles Paul and Peter seem to take a revolutionary stance when it comes to things of the church and the unity of all people in a spiritual sense. When it came to marriage, they don't seem quite as willing to undertake the overthrow of familial systems. On home matters, the apostles of old seemed comfortable continuing with a status quo, not trying to bring about any change.

If we study the surrounding verses on texts that relate to submissive marital relationships, we find a few other points. The first is a command for all believers to submit to one another, and later, for parents to obey children and slaves to obey masters. Because we are reading the Bible in the context of chapter and verse, it's easy to divide passages up and assume they are part of different ideals or thoughts when they aren't. These letters were sent out as one unified letter (without chapter or verse divisions). When it comes to the church, marriage, parents, and slaves, they were all ideas that related to a similar theme and ran together. The teachings on men and women, slaves, and children were all a part of an ancient societal code that governed Greek and Roman societies, kind of akin to the concepts of Confucius that were introduced in ancient China. They are related to household duties and responsibilities. Men were seen as the head of their households, which means they were responsible for finances, property acquisitions, governance, and were the legal right-holders when it came to societal representation, politics, and voting. To explain it in a way that is more understandable, men were given full legal status as governors of their immediate households, responsible for implementing and executing the laws of a nation therein. Along with such governance came the rights and privileges of being a man, doing that duty within society. In every household, women were subject to men, seen as their property, as were children and slaves. All three had about the same status under the legal observances of their cultures. Within this understanding, all three were required to yield themselves to the politics of their day, living under the existing systems.

We could say this is another aspect of New Testament ministry where the Apostles Paul and Peter encouraged their members to remain current with their cultures, just as they did when it came to matters of attire and public conduct. This doesn't mean they believed such was a rule in perpetuity, that the systems would never change, or that relationships between men and women and men and their households wouldn't evolve. They were giving advice, most likely to help keep Christians out of jail and avoid attracting unnecessary attention to themselves or their relationships in the hopes their lives would enable them to live their lives and continue to follow Christ.

Even within the confines of their words, believers are encouraged to submit one to another, as unto the Lord. It is also clarified that the head of all things is Christ, which means it was made explicitly clear the true head of everyone, no matter what laws or codes may be in place within a nation, is Christ Himself. This placed men in a submissive position to the Lord. In encouraging women to submit to their husbands, the Greek of the passage indicates it was in the same sense she would submit to any other believer. This means the so-called "yielding" of a woman wasn't to be in a special or unique context at home, but in the same regard and recognition that all believers are to submit to one another.

This might sound too simple of an explanation, so I will now give a more spiritual answer for those who won't find the historical context to be satisfying. The entirety of the passage was to teach about spiritual matters, those that related specifically to Christ and the church. By using marriage as a spiritual illustration, the apostles used imagery most familiar to those married in the first century. They were trying to teach us about unity: that in a place of marriage, there is a oneness that should be present, one that only comes from God because God was first, before we ever considered having a marriage. Just as we are one in marriage in a close, intimate setting (one that reflects love and respect) so too are we one with Christ in the church. The focus of the passage is not so much on the sacrifice of female submission as it is on the sacrifice of Christ, on the nature of the way that Christ gave Himself for the church with His own body. This is compared to the way men paid a bridal price for their wives, making a financial sacrifice to "pay" for the rights to his wife. It displayed the intense severity we should recognize Christ's redemption for us and our union with Him. By seeing Christ and the church in marriage, it provided a valuable imagery for believers to see Christ in themselves in a way they could easily understand.

I don't believe we properly understand the spiritual nature of marriage. Every Christian marriage should reflect the unity of Christ and the church, by which marital partners become a living type of the love Christ has for us and we have for Christ. This realization should force the debates over roles and power and control to cease. The purpose of these passages was never, ever to inspire argument and embitterment within people. In no marriage is anyone married to Jesus Christ Himself, thus some things must be clarified, worked out, and improved through time. They aren't here to cause division. They also do not give the right for any one partner to be inconsiderate or abusive toward the other. None of these things are present in the passages, nor are relevant to the discussion.

Teaching on the value of submission for all believers never goes out of vogue, or style. The submission of all believers is a part of the trust and unity of the church, and is something that, above all, every believer is called to do toward God. If we are Christians, we are learning to humble ourselves, esteem ourselves properly, and live for God. This must be done in marriage as much as anywhere else.

So yes, marriage in the context of the ancient codes is out of date and does not apply in the same way it did back then. This doesn't mean we throw out the passages. It means we strive in a greater way to understand what God wants to teach us through marriage. Because we are both growing spiritually and following the customs of our society, it is that much more important to reflect the principle of mutual submission in marriage and educate others on the spirituality of these passages.

Sarah called Abraham "Lord." Should I call my spouse the same?

In 1 Peter 3:5-6, Sarah is lauded as an example of submission. It states Sarah called her husband "lord" out of a sense of submission and respect:

For this is the way the holy women of the past who put their hope in God used to adorn themselves. They submitted themselves to their own husbands, like Sarah, who obeyed Abraham and called him her lord. You are her daughters if you do what is right and do not give way to fear.

When people are bored on social media, it's not uncommon to see the question, "Is it appropriate for women to call their husbands lord?" citing the passage above as their reference. It spawns arguments. It spawns discussion. It spawns disagreement. What is the answer to the question: should women call their spouses "lord" today?

I could answer this with a lot of rhetoric about times and things changing, but I think it is best to point out a couple of key things that help our understanding of the passage's context. If we understand the backdrop, it answers many questions about the appropriateness of such a term, especially in modern times.

Sarah was not the only one in the Bible who called her husband "lord," nor was she the only one to refer to another human being as "lord." "Lord" was a term of governorship or rulership extended to those who owned property and were head authorities over their estates. It is much like we would hear of "lords and ladies" of the manor in European history.

The title was not extended to everyone and was exclusively used in such this specific, limited context.

Sarah called Abraham "lord" because he was literally her lord in their culture. She had no rights and was deemed as property. As a result, Abraham was her literal ruler. He had the power to make decisions about her and he – not she – owned what we would classify today as their "marital property." Like others present on the property, she was part of his estate. Therefore, calling Abraham "lord" wasn't an oddity. It was a title of respect reflecting the times in which they lived. It showed honor to him as her societal and political dignitary and acknowledged such through culturally appropriate means.

The term "lord" as was used in the Bible doesn't apply in modern society. Most of us no longer live on huge family estates complete with slaves and servants. We are lucky to have an acre or two of property on which our house sits. Some of us don't even have that; we live in apartments or townhouses. To refer to someone as "lord" who was not in a governmental setting or a landowner was inappropriate, even in Biblical times. The term "lord" was not extended to Abraham because he was Sarah's husband, but because of his social status. It wasn't a casual term thrown around to cause trouble or ire and was certainly not used without proper context of due respect.

Beyond these facts, I must question the context by which we are implying Sarah's "submissiveness." It was Sarah's bright idea to bring Ishmael into this world, and Abraham complied with the idea. In the Isaac/Ishmael/Hagar/Sarah/Abraham craziness, we see Sarah pulling many of the strings: sending Hagar and Ishmael away, mistreating or abusing Hagar, and ultimately making the decision to have the two removed from the home permanently. It certainly doesn't sound like Sarah was just sitting around, saying "Yes, dear!" to every idea or desire Abraham had. Sarah was engaged in their lives and took authority where she could, whether it always had a positive ending. Sarah's imagery as "submissive" certainly doesn't match the image we have of it, today. It was nice of her to extend respect to Abraham, but she wasn't a mouse, either.

The passage tells us we are Sarah's daughters if we do what is right and don't give way to fear. It doesn't say women (even in the New Testament times) should call their husbands "lord." I would argue that in our modern day, calling someone "lord" has a lot more weight and association with worship than it did in ancient times. It's not appropriate to assign such titles of worship to human beings. We don't call property owners "lord" anymore. Since we associate such with worship today, to do so today is improper.

There are many ways we can express our respect and appreciation for a spouse besides using a title that causes confusion because its usage has changed. This passage is also a good example of why studying Scripture is so vitally important: cultures, times, word usages, and signs of honor and respect all change. If we don't understand these changes, we are missing part of the message of Scripture – especially as applies to us today.

Should Communion only be for Christians?

If you spend a lot of time on social media, it seems like there are as many opinions about communion as there are Christians. It's not uncommon to watch discussions descend into full-fledged arguments, often resulting in a lot of back-and-forth frustrations that don't help bridge the gap in understanding. With people on every side of the argument, the question remains: who is free to partake of communion?

In answering this question, there are a few different aspects that should be explored. I'll also say upfront there is no way to answer this question that will please all sides, especially when we take the time to examine the issue with consideration of the facts involved.

To understand the existing beliefs about communion, we must first understand what it is, as well as how people understand it. There are three different definitions of communion, as well as several subheadings that can also follow under each.

In its strictest, most literal definition, communion is a Christian rite that memorializes the death of Christ. During communion, some form of bread (unleavened or leavened) and wine or grape juice are blessed and shared with those present. Christians model this rite in Christ's command to "Do this in memory of Me" as found in the Gospels:

When the hour came, Jesus and His apostles reclined at the table. And He said to them, "I have eagerly desired to eat this Passover with you before I suffer. For I tell you, I will not eat it again until it finds fulfillment in the Kingdom of God."

After taking the cup, He gave thanks and said, "Take this and divide it among you. For I tell you I will not drink again from the fruit of the vine until the Kingdom of God comes."

And He took bread, gave thanks and broke it, and gave it to them, saying, "This is My body given for you; do this in remembrance of Me."

In the same way, after the supper He took the cup, saying, "This cup is the new covenant in My blood, which is poured out for you." (Matthew 26:14-20)

While they were eating, Jesus took bread, and when He had given thanks, He broke it and gave it to His disciples, saying, "Take it; this is My body."

Then He took a cup, and when He had given thanks, He gave it to them, and they all drank from it.

"This is My blood of the covenant, which is poured out for many," He said to them. *"Truly I tell you, I will not drink again from the fruit of the vine until that day when I drink it new in the Kingdom of God."*

When they had sung a hymn, they went out to the Mount of Olives. (Mark 14:22-26)

When the hour came, Jesus and His apostles reclined at the table. And He said to them, "I have eagerly desired to eat this Passover with you before I suffer. For I tell you, I will not eat it again until it finds fulfillment in the Kingdom of God."

After taking the cup, He gave thanks and said, "Take this and divide it among you. For I tell you I will not drink again from the fruit of the vine until the Kingdom of God comes."

And He took bread, gave thanks and broke it, and gave it to them, saying, "This is My body given for you; do this in remembrance of Me."

In the same way, after the supper he took the cup, saying, "This cup is the new covenant in My blood, which is poured out for you." (Luke 22:14-20)

From these three passages we learn the rite of Communion was instituted by Jesus Himself. It was done as part of His final Passover meal with His disciples. Jesus used what was on the table as part of the meal: unleavened bread and wine, using these two elements as symbols for the suffering and death He would soon endure for the sacrifice of our sins. The only people present at the dinner were Christ and the twelve who walked closely with Him throughout His ministry. This included Judas, who would betray Jesus a few hours later.

In some churches, communion is preceded or precluded with foot washing, which is found in the Gospel of John:

It was just before the Passover Festival. Jesus knew that the hour had come for Him to leave this world and go to the Father. Having loved His own who were in the world, He loved them to the end.

The evening meal was in progress, and the devil had already prompted Judas, the son of Simon Iscariot, to betray Jesus.

Jesus knew that the Father had put all things under His power, and that He had come from God and was returning to God; so He got up from the meal, took off His outer clothing, and wrapped a towel around his waist. After that, He poured water into a basin and began to wash His disciples' feet, drying them with the towel that was wrapped around Him.

He came to Simon Peter, who said to Him, "Lord, are you going to wash my feet?"

Jesus replied, "You do not realize now what I am doing, but later you will understand."

"No," said Peter, "You shall never wash my feet."

Jesus answered, "Unless I wash you, you have no part with Me."

"Then, Lord," Simon Peter replied, "not just my feet but my hands and my head as well!"

Jesus answered, "Those who have had a bath need only to wash their feet; their whole body is clean. And you are clean, though not every one of you." For He knew who was going to betray Him, and that was why He said not every one was clean.

When He had finished washing their feet, He put on his clothes and returned to His place. "Do you understand what I have done for you?" He asked them. "You call me 'Teacher' and 'Lord,' and rightly so, for that is what I am. Now that I, your Lord and Teacher, have washed your feet, you also should wash one another's feet. I have set you an example that you should do as I have done for you. Very truly I tell you, no servant is greater than his master, nor is a messenger greater than the one who sent him. Now that you know these things, you will be blessed if you do them. (John 13:1-17)

Thus, communion is, first and foremost, a memorial, or

remembrance, of the sacrifice of Christ. It teaches us about being a servant; about the sacrificial aspect of love, seldom spoke of in many circles. It serves to unite us with Him in His death, ultimately acknowledging that if we die with Him, we also rise with Him. We partake of communion because it honors Him and connects us to Him.

Communion can also be the specific church service or occasion by which we partake of this memorial. It may be done at church weekly or occasionally, at a church meal or fellowship, a wedding or funeral, or other occasion by which two are three are gathered in His Name.

Another definition of communion relates to the rite itself: the idea of unity and common participation as symbolized by the Communion experience. When we partake of communion we are not just uniting to Jesus as a person, but to His Body as well – the church as a whole. For this reason, when and where we choose to take communion matters. When we take communion, we are in communion with both the immediate and universal body of believers.

The last definition, also related to the previous one, is the specific relationship that exists during certain churches, ministries, or denominations that are acknowledged as legitimate and accepted by one another. These groups all hold tenets of faith or certain authority in common, acknowledging the legitimacy of a group.

The Bible also outlines personal requirements for partaking in communion in 1 Corinthians 11:17-32:

In the following directives I have no praise for you, for your meetings do more harm than good. In the first place, I hear that when you come together as a church, there are divisions among you, and to some extent I believe it. No doubt there have to be differences among you to show which of you have God's approval. So then, when you come together, it is not the Lord's Supper you eat, for when you are eating, some of you go ahead with your own private suppers. As a result, one person remains hungry and another gets drunk. Don't you have homes to eat and drink in? Or do you despise the church of God by humiliating those who have nothing? What shall I say to you? Shall I praise you? Certainly not in this matter!

For I received from the Lord what I also passed on to you: The Lord Jesus, on the night He was betrayed, took bread, and when He had given thanks, He broke it and said, "This is My body, which is for you; do this in remembrance of Me." In the same way, after supper he took the cup, saying, "This cup is the new covenant in My blood; do this, whenever you drink it, in remembrance of Me." For whenever you eat this bread and drink this cup, you proclaim the Lord's death until He comes.

So then, whoever eats the bread or drinks the cup of the Lord in an unworthy manner will be guilty of sinning against the body and blood of the Lord. Everyone ought to examine themselves before they eat of the bread and drink from the cup. For those who eat and drink without discerning the body of Christ eat and drink judgment on themselves. That is why many among you are weak and sick, and a number of you have fallen asleep. But if we were more discerning with regard to ourselves, we would not come under such judgment. Nevertheless, when we are judged in this way by the Lord, we are being disciplined so that we will not be finally condemned with the world.

There's a lot going on in this passage, much of which I will explain later. We learn here the criteria for communion:

- Not showing up drunk or high (intoxicated)
- Do not partake of communion because of physical

hunger or gluttony
- Refrain from receiving communion in an unworthy manner
- Discern one's own motives and spiritual state of being prior to partaking of communion.

There are two major Christian perspectives on communion: the first is closed communion, which upholds the idea that communion is only open to specific members of a church or denomination. Roman Catholicism, Orthodoxy, and some assorted Protestant denominations practice closed communion. In Roman Catholicism and Orthodoxy, only baptized members of their respective churches are permitted to receive communion. There are some Protestant denominations (not many in modern times but still a few) that only allow members to receive communion if they have a certain moral standing within the church community. Traditionally, such members were given a "token" and could not receive communion if they did not have one. Closed communion exists because the aforementioned denominations see communion as more than a personal choice. To them, it represents unity with the beliefs a group has about communion, the leadership of that organization, and the unity with other members who feel the same way.

While closed communion was once a denominational standard, now it is often regarded as an elitist or exclusionary practice. In favor of closed communion, open communion is now a Protestant norm. In open communion, participation is open to any baptized Christian, regardless of denomination. In many instances, participants are encouraged to examine their hearts prior to receiving as is commanded in 1 Corinthians 11:28-29. There is often no teaching on what one is called to examine or what should preclude one from participation. The focus is, instead, on communion being open and a matter of personal conscience.

Even though open communion is typically specified as open to any Christian, many denominations often opt to open communion to all whether Christian or not. They argue that participating in communion might be someone's first open door to accepting Christ, and if Judas was present and received communion, so should everyone else, regardless of their theological alignments.

Given these two very different views of communion, what is the proper approach to communion?

In over twenty years as a Christian, I have never heard of someone becoming a Christian because they received communion as a non-Christian. While I won't discount it might have happened at some point in time, I don't know of any examples myself. I will also say I question the use of communion – the very memorial of the way Christ gave Himself for His people – as an evangelism tool. There are many other ways we can extend the love of God to those who don't believe, and I'd argue that all religions have specific practices that are off-limits to those who don't adhere to the beliefs of each specific group.

I believe that before we partake of communion, we need to understand communion. It's not just a snack service in the middle of church. It is a sacred rite, something that needs to have value to those who partake. Just as baptism unites us to Christ's death, so does communion. Just as baptism unites us to the body, so communion unites us to the body. Communion helps us understand our life in Christ as well as our life and place in the church. If we don't understand the spiritual meaning of communion, we are going to approach it with an attitude of entitlement: I am entitled to take communion because it's my right, rather than I am welcome to take communion because God has invited me to this table.

If we understand communion, we can better understand why the Apostle Paul warned the Corinthian church about receiving communion in an unworthy manner. Communion isn't about us and our right to do things but remembering Christ's sacrifice for our salvation. The Corinthian church neither understood the principle of communion nor of uniting them with God and one another. Instead, they used their communion services to fuel divisions – discriminating against the poor, getting drunk, refusing to eat, behaving badly, and failing to love one another – rather than fostering true fellowship. They made communion about themselves and their needs instead of about Jesus and uniting one to another.

Before we argue we aren't as "bad" as the Corinthians were, we need to step back and examine ourselves: Are we fostering the spirit of true communion in ourselves, or are we participating in division? Are we embracing what Christ died for us to have, or are we using our faith to serve as a stumbling block? Do we recognize our faith is bigger than just about us and Jesus, or are we worried about our entitlements and rights?

I advocate for a different understanding of communion than "open" or "closed." The problem isn't communion, but how we understand it and how we see our relationship with the body of Christ. The Corinthian church approached communion from a self-centered perspective: it was about who could receive the most rather than considering others present. I do believe communion is for Christians, but I also don't have the time to police the communion table and monitor the worthiness of participants based on my own personal standards. I believe we should teach on communion, and I also believe we should consider our own worthiness before we receive. Our "worthiness" isn't there to nullify the grace of God or damn anyone to hell, but to cause each person to pause and realize communion involves both the individual and the entire body of believers at the same time. Receiving is a matter of personal conscience, one that can be shaped by proper understanding of communion and education about the true meaning of the spiritual rite. If Christians desire communion to be a respectable Christian practice, we must first respect it ourselves.

Do Faith and Feminism Align?

There's no doubt that faith and feminism are often a controversial bag. They are often seen as total opposites. Is this accurate? Would we say that feminism is a contradiction of faith? The answer might surprise you!

First, let's define what a feminist, or an adherent of "feminism," is. A feminist is defined as someone who believes in the social and political equality of men and women. In modern feminism, feminists typically uphold the equality of all genders, not just restricting equality to binaries. In other words, a feminist believes that all people are equal, and men should not be given partial treatment due to the fact they are men. There are many different systems of feminism, some more extreme than others, some more moderate, that all adhere to the same basic principle, but vary in how they feel such can be accomplished.

One of the reasons many find feminism threatening is because of what they think it is, when it's not that, at all. To help our understanding, let's define what feminism is not:

- Feminism is not the belief that all men should be eradicated.
- Feminism does not believe women are superior to men.
- Feminism does not advocate women become men or have to be like men.
- Feminism does not believe women have no flaws or issues within themselves.
- Feminism doesn't think it is a bad thing to be a man.
- Feminism doesn't think the Bible is archaic, or that

faith is a bad thing to have.

- Feminism doesn't believe it's wrong to be a mother or to make good choices for one's family.

I don't question whether there are people sometimes who malign and misinterpret the ideas of feminism based on their own interpretation of it. This is true of any group, movement, and ideological platform. There are plenty of people who malign the message of Christianity, but we don't refrain from calling ourselves Christians because a few people take things to the extreme. The same is true with feminism. The concept that all are equal, and no one should experience gender discrimination are important and liberating precepts for women. It gives freedom and the mobility to follow wherever God leads rather than feeling limited and restricted based on outdated gender roles.

The first feminists were all Christian women. They desired to be ministers but were denied access to all-male seminaries. Their response was to start their own seminaries and familiarize themselves with the same curriculum and knowledge, educating themselves better than the men did. Through information and education, these women fought with knowledge and presented themselves more than competent and able to do exactly what God equipped them to do. As the work went on, these women began to advocate for different issues of their day: women's rights to equal property ownership and distribution, the abolition of slavery, the right to vote, educational opportunities, alcohol temperance, and equality in marriage.

As time went on, feminism took on new resurgence and ideals. In later waves of feminism, the movements had a more secular base than a Christian foundation. Modern feminists advocate for many of the same things, plus accesses to health care, women's representation in government, social justice, universal equality, legislative reform on issues that pertain to women (such as rape laws or domestic violence), gender equality, and yes, there are still those voices that advocate for equality in church.

I don't know a single Christian woman who would denounce the basic principles of feminism. While not all feminists agree on specific issues (such as access to abortion or details of legislative change) all agree that women should have the same basic rights to things that male counterparts have. It seeks to erase the concept of gender specified norms: that women must stay home and clean a house and cook while a man must go to work and earn money. There's nothing wrong with any of these things, but there is something wrong when society assigns us a value of how well we can do them without options or choices. How we may live to accomplish this goal may vary, but that is part of feminism's message, as well. Feminism opens the door for us to discover a sense of ourselves we might not have otherwise: whether it's through career, motherhood, stay-at-home childcare, a stay-at-home dad, a female CEO, a woman who earns more than her spouse, a single woman, living and thriving as a single aromantic asexual, being a trans-woman, career choices, educational opportunities, and so on. Through feminism, we have options rather than regulations.

So yes, faith and feminism are aligned. As believers, we should seek to implement and uphold equality, not just in society, but in our congregations and ministries, as well. We should give people of every gender the opportunity to serve, to pursue their callings, and to feel they have a voice and a relevance in their faith. Both faith and feminism bring us right back to the reality of choices, decision-making, and options. Without feminism, it would be far more difficult to pursue whatever it is we feel called to pursue. If you want the freedom to be who God has created you to be as a woman, feminism is, undeniably, one of the things God has used to help make that possible.

How can I connect with God in prayer?

Prayer is essential and foundational in our relationship with God. Many people also find it one of the most challenging. We live in a world that talks about communication, but in all our speaking, texting, emailing, calling, faxing, and sharing, we often miss the messages received through these means. People complain of loneliness and isolation. It would appear that in all our communicating, we aren't connecting.

Prayer is a connection for communication. It is having a conversation with God, much like you might have with someone else you might know. If you love your friends and family you desire to talk to them, to spend time with them and share with them. You don't only talk about what's bothering you because you seek a solution, but because sharing has value and benefit. You share what brings you joy because others can share your happiness along with you. We don't just communicate with those we love for answers or directions, but to share something with them. On the inverse, we also listen and receive what we love express or share because we enjoy being with them.

If you are having issues with prayer, I am going to guess it is probably because you think prayer must be something specific to be authentic. When we look at more traditional examples of prayer, it's easy to think we should pray exactly like they do to get it right. We've received the concept that prayer is a display of personal piety instead of just communication, and there's a way to "pray wrong." None of this is the case. There is no reason to believe your prayers are ineffective, wrong, or bad. It's just a matter of where to start, and how to approach it.

The Scriptures list many different types, possible postures, and ideas for prayer. If you aren't sure where to start when studying prayer, getting lost in the topic is a possibility. There are many different forms of prayer because there are many different situations and circumstances throughout the Bible that drew people to prayer. That means there isn't a "right way" or a "wrong way" to pray. For a starting point, Jesus' words on prayer are some of the most well-known throughout the world. Found in Matthew 6:9-13, they read:

"This, then, is how you should pray:

"'Our Father in heaven,
hallowed be Your Name,
Your Kingdom come,
Your will be done,
*   on earth as it is in heaven.*
Give us today our daily bread.
And forgive us our debts,
*   as we also have forgiven our debtors.*
And lead us not into temptation,
*   but deliver us from the evil one.'"*

This practical format tells us "how to pray" in the Scriptures. It's not that we must recite what He said word-for-word (although there's nothing wrong with that), but these are the things most central to us in our lives: God, the Kingdom of God, the will of God, our physical sustenance, forgiveness, ability to forgive, avoiding temptation, and deliverance from all evil. When you look at prayer through this lens, it covers an entire expanse of life issues: of those that set us right, away from things that lead us into wrong paths, and for us to have our basic needs met. It emphasizes communication, covering our entire lives, and opening the door for us to discuss more.

When going before God in prayer, try a simple exercise that might help you to relax and communicate with God more effectively. Find a quiet place and put on some soft music (or if you prefer silence, as some do, sit silently). Breathe deeply and slowly. Instead of trying to find words, let whatever you want to say to God come out, naturally. Instead of focusing so much on saying what you think "sounds right," just be honest with God. We can have assurance He already knows everything, so whatever we say isn't going to come as a huge, unbearable shock. This is your time to communicate with God what is most purposeful – and important – to you.

MY FORMER CHURCH OBSERVED MANY RULES AND REGULATIONS. I STILL STRUGGLE WITH LEGALISM. WHAT DO YOU SUGGEST?

Legalism is the belief that following an excessive number of rules and regulations is essential to maintaining one's salvation. Most legalistic churches won't tell you that such rules are required to be saved, but if you are truly saved you will follow their list of rules. There are several reasons why this doctrinal position becomes problematic: it leads to self-righteousness, it causes confusion about salvation and the nature of grace, and it is very rare that people can follow the vast, complex number of regulations to the letter. It can feel confusing and often, it often feels oppressive.

Legalism takes on a whole new dimension when someone, for whatever reason, is automatically discounted from salvation due to an inability to follow a rule or rules. There may be an expectation may be for someone to deny themselves or follow additional rules, such as if someone is female or LGBTQ+. The message we often receive is that we should be uncomfortable in our own skin.

The darker side of legalism is that such patterns don't magically disappear because we intellectually and spiritually understand they are harmful to us. Just as there was a process to learn the rules, there's also a process to unlearn them. With all things, doing so takes time.

I believe we are not just called to overcome our histories but reconcile ourselves with them. What this means – beyond the idea of overcoming or conquering – is that we accept our past for what it was, the good and the bad, and the indifferent. We often start to hit walls and encounter stagnation when working to overcome legalism because stepping away from such a system confuses us. When we step back and view it in hindsight, things seem different. At first, we see the level of legalism we experienced, often in overdrive. It's all we see and can be difficult to process.

Then, as time goes by, we start to process our history differently. It might take a few months or a few years, but our experience is dotted with both good memories along with the more difficult ones. We knew some good people, we had some great times, we worshiped God as we understood Him at the time. It wasn't all good or all bad, but a decidedly mixed bag that makes the process suddenly more complicated.

I mention these facts because reconciling our history is a process. We were indoctrinated and we lived an entire life that went along with that indoctrination. We put what we were taught into practice, applied the ideas, followed them, and obeyed our leaders. They were part of us as much as we were part of them. It can be hard to separate it from the greater life we lived, always tempting to overemphasize one aspect or another.

What I would say is work toward your reconciliation within yourself. You did the best you could at the time and those who were in your life also did the best they knew how to do, even if it wasn't perfect. It's all right that things were what they were, and that you have moved on and now see things differently. Apply your newly found freedom and embrace forgiveness.

As you do these things, open yourself up to learn new doctrine and new applications for your faith. Don't fall into the extreme of thinking it's better to abandon everything. Be open to learning a new way, still holding to what you know is true. Make a point to apply what you learn along with what you already know and allow the two to endow you with power to continue.

In all things, keep going. Keep growing. Keep expanding out. Keep exploring new territories. Keep moving into new places. Keep learning. Keep being everything that makes you who you are as a believer in Christ. Most of all, be patient with yourself. We all kick ourselves over some of the things we believed, did, and said, back when we didn't know any better. Now we know; then we didn't. Reconcile it. Let it be what brought you to where you are now and learn to embrace that as you move forward.

What is the "Spirit of Jezebel?"

The "spirit of Jezebel" is a catch-all term many preachers use to describe any individual who proves antithetical to ministry operation or advancement. The associated behaviors include sexual enticement, enchantment, "religious spirits," usurping of authority, control, dominance, manipulation, deception, confusion, intimidation, and especially, interested in usurping or overthrowing male authority. Whenever you hear the term used, it is employed by leaders who are "warning" about such a person or labeling someone as such a person. There are books, programs, articles, blogs, and yes, social media posts on the existence of and situations caused by this so-called spirit, but I believe the question remains: just what is it?

The "spirit of Jezebel" is nothing because it does not exist. To explain, I think it is better to go back and explain why such is not only false – it is dangerous.

I first heard the term "spirit of Jezebel" used around 2011. It was a very difficult and complicated time in my ministry. I had people who met the description around me, thus causing me to take interest in this vague spirit's description. The people around me weren't interested in taking over my entire ministry as much as running it behind-the-scenes. They desired to have a special kind of relationship with me; one other members of the ministry did not have. It was not sexually or physically inappropriate, but I dealt with several people who desired to influence my ministry through their financial giving, advice I did not want, and behaving inappropriately (like children) when they did not get their way. They were awful to deal with, and it seemed like everywhere I looked, there they were in my midst. Most reached a point of no return and stormed off the ministry scene to do their "own thing," all of which crashed and burned, taking their manipulative means (such as their giving) with them.

So, when I first heard about the "spirit of Jezebel," I jumped on the bandwagon for a very short period because I experienced the sting of people trying to control my work from within. However...it didn't take long before I became uncomfortable with the label. Something didn't feel right, and I did some further investigation and talked to a new minister under my ministry about it. After reviewing the Scriptures about Jezebel, Ahab, and their crazy reign over Israel we were able to see the behaviors often attributed to the "spirit of Jezebel" were not part of her governance. There's no question she was an ungodly woman and did not rightly govern, but there is no evidence of the accusations made about Jezebel in connection with this mystery spirit.

Jezebel was a Biblical figure during the reign of King Ahab, leader of the nation of Israel for about twenty-two years. We read about Jezebel in 1 Kings 16, 18-21 and 2 Kings 9. The Scriptures tell us Ahab deliberately sought out Jezebel, daughter of the king of the Sidonians, because she was a pagan idolater and not a daughter of Israel. While many who speak on the "spirit of Jezebel" focus on the character of Jezebel, the presence of Jezebel in Israel's history doesn't speak so much of her as it does of Ahab and what he desired to accomplish as ruler of the nation. He was so wicked and astray in his beliefs, he desired to rebel against God and the laws of Israel by deliberately marrying a woman who wasn't a Hebrew. Ahab sought her out, made an alliance with a pagan nation, and then brought her into his rule, all while she was somewhere else minding her own business.

Jezebel's governance over Israel was given to her. She did not usurp or steal any authority; it was bestowed upon her as ruler and queen. If there is anything we can say, Jezebel was the model of that perfect balance between submission and authority. She did nothing without the consent of the king, who also happened to be her husband. She stepped up to do it for him when he wanted someone else to do it on his behalf. Nothing says she tried to take over as king or dethrone Ahab. They moved in a perfect rhythm to establish and complete spiritual chaos throughout Israel at that time in history.

Not one time was the Prophet Elijah sent to deliver a message to Jezebel: she wasn't the king. Elijah was sent to Ahab because he was the king and was the one responsible for bringing Jezebel (and this mess) into Israel in the first place. Ahab was the problem; Jezebel was a casualty and co-conspirator, using her husband's laziness and manipulativeness for her own ends. The issues Israel had, though, were not due to Jezebel. They were foundational issues, caused by Ahab.

We have zero evidence to suggest Jezebel was ever a sexually seductive adulterer. She never overthrew her husband's authority, although it is safe to say she might have been the more skillful leader on an interpersonal level. Jezebel was in no way manipulative, dominating, controlling, confusing, intimidating, or deceiving. When people talk about having a "religious spirit" (another thing that does not exist), they use the term to indicate someone is legalistic. There is nothing that stands to say Jezebel was rigid or inflexible, because she was multi-faceted and busy doing her husband's dirty work in many different areas. Jezebel was exactly who she was, brought into Israel because of who she was, and did exactly the things she was comfortable doing.

There is absolutely no Scriptural evidence to say Jezebel is a "spirit." The term "spirit of Jezebel" is found nowhere in Scripture. On the list of spirits in Scripture, Jezebel is not listed, even among spirits or demons identified with a name. Because Jezebel was a person, when she died her identity died with her. There is one reference of Jezebel in the New Testament, found in Revelation 2:20:

Nevertheless, I have this against you: You tolerate that woman Jezebel, who calls herself a prophet. By her teaching she misleads my servants into sexual immorality and the eating of food sacrificed to idols.

The passage does not state they tolerated a woman with the spirit of Jezebel, but a woman calling herself a prophet identified as "Jezebel," who was clearly an idolater. There are only a few possibilities as to what this passage means: it might have indicated her name was Jezebel, or it might have been a reference to the presence of this false prophet at work in the church. To compare her to Jezebel would mean the church sought her out, followed her false teaching, brought her into the church, and she led and instructed them in the ways of idolatry, just as Ahab did with Jezebel. This doesn't mean the false prophet had a "spirit" of Jezebel, but that her role became like Jezebel's in her day.

Where did we get the idea that Jezebel is a "spirit" associated with all these characteristics that have nothing to do with Jezebel herself? It turns out the term "Jezebel" goes back to American slavery and Jim Crow. It was a slur used against African American women and women of color in general to blame and assign subordination to them. Women of color were (and still sometimes are) stereotyped as being hypersexual, untrustworthy with men, rebellious, and insubordinate to authority. Nowadays, the term is used to describe any woman who is viewed as sexually "loose," morally indiscriminate, or politically or socially ambitious, but the association with such goes back to the Jim Crow stereotype against women of color. The term is a racist and sexist slur, and there is no redeeming quality to use this term in modern society.

Most individuals who promote the existence of this imaginary spirit don't offer a lot of advice on how to deal with it, cast it out, or address it. Their commentary is often highly dramatic and if I might say so, has a shrill quality to it. They sound like individuals with a strong desire to control their image and run their ministries as the central focus, rather than embodying servanthood and spiritual guidance therein. They don't want anyone to come along and challenge them, and they decide everyone who challenges them has the "spirit of Jezebel." They have difficulty keeping steady followers and often embody the very characteristics they accuse others of having.

Just because the spirit of Jezebel doesn't exist doesn't mean we won't ever encounter or meet someone who might have certain negative characteristics associated with the "spirit of Jezebel," such as manipulation, control, or deception. It's important we identify such behaviors and conduct ourselves accordingly. As ministers, we must prepare ourselves for people who do come to make trouble to protect the vision God has given to us. This is different from spiritual paranoia (where we think everyone who is different, doesn't agree, or is in a different place than us is somehow out to overthrow us and our work). God hasn't called us to have subjects; He has called us to be servants. If we look at our role in this way, it allows for the human differences we will encounter. It helps us to better assess spiritual issues, character issues, and personality traits rather than branding everyone like this, that, or something else.

Calling someone "Jezebel" or labeling someone as having "the spirit of Jezebel," is wrong. Its context and usage today are not Biblical, and it is a racist and demeaning slur against women. It's an insult. We should not use, nor embody, culturally derogatory terms in church. It doesn't become spiritually acceptable to do so just because someone slaps the word "spirit" in front of it. Don't use it.

If you are interested in true healing and deliverance ministry, I recommend educating yourself in Biblical definitions of spirits, demons, and the difference between the two. You will quickly find Jezebel is nowhere to be found. You will also discover that such genuine work is far more involved than the drama of demon-hunting we often see pursued today. If this is where you feel called, avoid the pop culture approach to spirituality and dig deep. It is there you will find out the truth about such issues.

SECTION 2:

SORTING OUT MINISTRY

You yourselves are our letter,
written on our hearts,
known and read by everyone.
You show that you are a letter from Christ,
the result of our ministry, written not with ink
but with the Spirit of the living God, not on tablets
of stone but on tablets of human hearts.

Such confidence we have through Christ
before God.
Not that we are competent in ourselves to claim
anything for ourselves, but our competence
comes from God.
He has made us competent as ministers
of a new covenant—not of the letter
but of the Spirit; for the letter kills,
but the Spirit gives life.

(2 Corinthians 3:2-6)

How do I know if I am called to ministry?

Believe it or not, this is one of those questions that all people have, regardless of gender. I wish it was a conversation we felt more comfortable having in church. Our silence on this issue has made it hard to discuss and even harder for many to discern. That means many wait to discover their calling much longer than they should. When churches plan various classes, services, and retreats, they are not planning their events with the goal of helping someone discern or develop a call into ministry. Most church programs are designed to help lay members (those who are not in ministry) discover purpose and spiritual insight into their lives, as their lives are. This means if you are discerning a call into ministry, you will probably not find spiritual guidance or advice in an average Sunday sermon or a church event. What will most likely happen is you will have more questions and more to think about without helping you discern the specifics you seek.

Answering this specific question is difficult for me. Not knowing you and the unique elements of your relationship with God means I am not sure how to answer the question for you, at least not as specific as you might like. The way you discern a call to ministry relies heavily on your own spiritual interaction with God. You will best discern your call in the way God speaks to you and manifests Himself to you. It may come at any time and will, most likely, come because of an experience or in combination with one.

For example: if you are teaching a Sunday School class, you may be preparing for it or even teaching it when God reveals that you will teach beyond your Sunday School classroom. You may have a vision of you teaching a large audience. Maybe as you are putting together your lessons, God will show you writing a book or compiling many lessons. However you find your service to God, there you will find your purpose and calling in ministry if that is what God calls you to do.

If you are questioning your call to ministry, I would recommend seeking God's face in the way that you do most often. Listen for His voice. If that isn't something you are familiar with, I recommend doing some Scripture study into the different ways that God speaks to us. According to the Scriptures, God speaks to us:

- Audibly
- Angelic encounters
- Nature
- The inner voice (sometimes called witness) of the Holy Spirit
- Dreams, signs, and visions
- Prophecy
- Word of wisdom/word of knowledge
- Wise counsel
- Difficulties
- Whoever God so desires to speak through
- Scripture

Watch for the different ways that God speaks in your own life. Maybe you hear from God audibly or through dreams or visions, or even in your difficulties. No matter how God speaks to you, you can learn to attune to that voice so you are able to figure out just what God has to say to you about ministry. It's also advisable to talk to a trusted leader who can give you more specific advice based on their knowledge of your spiritual life and your current walk with God. That's what leaders are there for, and a good leader will help you to hear that voice of God and direct you with education and information as to where to head next with the steps to ministry discernment.

I HAVE A MINISTRY CALL, BUT NO ONE SEEMS TO BELIEVE ME. WHAT AM I DOING WRONG?

When we are first called to ministry, it is exciting. You probably experienced a certain level of spiritual awe and amazement when you came to accept the call of God on your life. At first, it was probably something between you and God, something that was part of the unique relationship you have with Him. Then, at a certain point, you couldn't keep it all to yourself anymore; you had to tell someone else. As the word started to get around, you probably encountered people who weren't quite as excited about your call as you were. They might have raised doubts, questioned what you had to do or say that was of relevance, or put you down because of something you have done in your life. That initial excitement waned, and has now been replaced by voices of doubt, all of which sound much like the people who didn't respond with excitement to the idea of your call.

It's not uncommon to experience other's doubts when you first announce a ministry call. When doubts arise (especially if those doubts are from people close to us), it can make one feel they are all alone. That's not the case, and what you are going through is part of the difficult road of being in ministry. Yes, ministry is a blessing, but it is also a big responsibility, and it can be a difficult experience. Part of accepting a ministerial call is accepting this reality of the work, and it is often something we experience out of the gate. We expect those around us to be happy and supportive, and sometimes, that is just not the case.

There are a lot of possible reasons as to why others around you aren't supportive of your new call to ministry.

The first is that the call is new. It being new, they are not sure how it is going to fit in with their concept of you and the way you fit in their lives. Ministry means change, and it doesn't just mean change for you, but for everyone around you. The second possibility is that others are very familiar with you, especially in the context of the person you were for a long period of time. They don't understand how that person can now be in ministry. When people are very close to us, they can conjure up past hurts, wounds, or misdeeds and use them against us, even though doing such isn't right. Sometimes people just can't fathom who we are and where we are going now because they haven't let go of what happened before. The third possibility is they might not know how to respond to your calling. Sometimes people aren't very knowledgeable or experienced with these things, and that can lead to judgment or disapproval of what they don't understand. Disbelief can translate to judgment, and sometimes judgment looks a lot like not supporting someone else's undertaking.

What I would say is you probably aren't doing anything wrong. You are excited and hoping and believing others would share in that excitement with you. There might be times when you might not do everything right or according to protocol, but that is to be understood. That doesn't disqualify you from ministry or having a call, it just means the responsibility of helping you learn what to do and how to do it goes to those in your life who are more experienced. There is probably a lot for you to learn, and it is my prayer that God will connect you with those who will help you to develop into the minister God has called you to be.

As for the disbelief of others, don't let it stop you; let it reconnect you. Take a deep breath and ask God to connect you to those who can help you and support what you are doing. Be open to different forms of support and instruction and see to it that you are spiritually connected to a good leader who can help you through this difficult part of your spiritual walk. Most importantly, keep listening to and trusting God, and don't ever give up on what you know He has revealed. He is there for you in all situations and can bring you through any difficulties that you will face.

Where Do I Start in Ministry?

Where you start in ministry depends on your circumstances, level of education and experience in ministry, and the personal and spiritual situations you find yourself in at current. I would encourage you to do some self-examination, as well as talking with your leader (or a trusted mentor if you don't have a leader yet) to establish and evaluate just where you are in the different steps of ministry progress.

The first thing to clarify is if you feel called to minister or feel called to ministry. These are two different things, and I will explain the difference to help your process. Being called to minister means you feel called to a sense of ministering duty, desiring to be more involved and active in your church or community as one who wants to proclaim the Gospel through action. In other words, you feel called to service. This is often a starting place for many in ministry, where people start to hear from God and hear the call to assume greater leadership work and position within the sphere of spiritual authority. Whether or not you believe you are called to have more authority within a ministerial context, I believe every leader must first hear the call to minister. You can gain insight into your spiritual calling through the call to minister, because through working in different aspects of service, you are able to learn a great deal about yourself and where your strengths, spiritual gifts, and abilities best lie.

Whether you feel called to minister or to ministry (as a call to ministry also involves a call to minister), the first stop on any ministry journey should always be the work of helps. The ministry of helps relates to any sort of lay membership work in the church that is completed on a volunteer basis. If you are involved in a spiritual community, you are probably aware there are many ways you can be involved in church. Helps include things such as assisting on the altar during service, cleaning the church, helping with the nursery, teaching Sunday School, working in the audio/visual department, street witnessing, ushering, singing in the choir or the worship team, dance ministry, or other works that are a part of the general function of the church. If you don't have experience in helps ministry, it is the best place to start, no matter what your call may be long-term.

This means if you are not connected to a church or a ministry, now is the time to seek God about connection with a godly, mature leader who is able to help you through your ministry process. It is possible you will eventually move on, but that is not the mentality you should have right now. In looking for a leader, it's important to be properly matched for the work you seek to do, recognizing leadership order and structure. If you aren't to the point where you have the experience and are ready to lead on your own, a leader with a history of training other leaders and helping to provide the needed experience to get from where you are to where you seek to go is crucial. If you are ready to lead on your own, having completed all the relevant steps, then you need a leader with a good history of working with leaders who are serving on-the-job and providing any necessary training gaps that might exist.

The next thing I would recommend is learning all you can about whatever ministry work you feel called to do. There are a few possibilities when it comes to ministry work. Some of the work is licensed and ordained, some are just licensed, and some are neither. If you desire to be of service but you don't feel called to a specific ministry office, the best option is one of the appointments of bishop, elder, or deacon. These three works, often misunderstood, are works of leadership service there to assist ministers of the Ephesians 4:11 ministry in a specific work. Bishops assist apostles, elders assist pastors, and deacons assist everyone. If this is something that might interest you, it is important to step up and speak with your leader about it. These works are "in ministry" and it is understood that in by serving these positions, you do so within the boundaries of the ministry you are part of, not on your own. Sometimes doing independent ministry and appointment work within another ministry is an option, but for that step, you would have to discuss such with your leader.

If you feel called to walk in a specific leadership work that God has called you to outside of an existing church or ministry, it is most advisable you learn about the Ephesians 4:11 ministry works and all that goes along with them. The ministry offices of apostle, prophet, evangelist, pastor, and teacher provide the essential foundation of ministry formation within the whole church. These offices are each different, specific works that handle different areas of leadership over the entire Body of Christ. Some of what they do is similar; some are different; some overlaps; and some are unique. Without getting into the specifics of what each work does, learning about these works is an important part of understanding how ministries work together and the responsibilities and duties of each office. No matter what office you may be called to, you will be called to work with other ministers in ministry, so learning about their call and responsibilities will help you to recognize your place, as well.

I also recommend ministry educational training, such as seminary, Bible school, or an equivalency of some sort. If a traditional Bible college or seminary is too expensive or you have reasons why attending a traditional school isn't a right fit, there are many other options for training. For example, Apostolic Covenant Theological Seminary operates a complete distance seminary program, available at both graduate and doctorate levels. Sometimes churches have small leadership training programs or Bible schools available within their congregations or extend them to their region or state. There are many programs available online. Just because one is called to ministry doesn't mean one doesn't need any sort of education, and good training can go a long way in the process of ministry establishment and success.

The last step to starting a ministry involves learning the ins and outs of what you need to do to legally establish your work, wherever you may be. Whether it is obtaining non-profit or charitable status, there is some heavy work involved in preparing a business package, the necessary media information to compose a press or media kit, and the needed information to budget and maintain your ministry finances, especially as your ministry grows. Sometimes people seek out a preparer or other individual to help with such steps, but even with help, you will still have to provide your group's basic information to whoever prepares your plan for you.

I would recommend three books for your journey: *Ministry School Boot Camp: Training For Helps Ministries, Appointments, and Beyond* (Righteous Pen Publications, 2014), *Ministry Officer Candidate School: Foundations for Christian Leadership* (Righteous Pen Publications, 2025), and *About My Father's Business: Professional Ministry For Kingdom Leaders* (Righteous Pen Publications, 2014) in order to provide some information on different options for ministering and ministry throughout the church. These books will help provide foundational information on everything: service, ministry specifics, and business guidelines, all designed and used as teaching resources for those interested in starting out in or expanding in ministry, however that may manifest for you.

WHERE CAN I FIND A SPIRITUAL FELLOWSHIP THAT FEEDS ME AS A LEADER?

When I first started work on this book, I answered this question very differently from how I will answer it today. My answer to this question? The spiritual fellowship you need is in the church, from a combination of sources: first from the local congregation you lead, and also from a network of leadership support that is found in a combination of places. Getting to this point is the challenge and starts with some basic principles we often ignore.

What you are experiencing is an aspect of ministry many have explored, but seldom resolved. When I was much younger in ministry, the answer to the problem was to create leadership networks by which leaders were connected to both a primary leadership covering and other leaders under that leader. In theory, it should have been a great solution to the problem: leaders found someone to help them as a leader, they found other leaders to fellowship with and connect to, and everyone was the better for it, right?

What we wound up doing was twofold. We created an infinite number of small networks that often did nothing more than spend a lot of money and never connect with one another and a generation of spoiled laity that gave no thought or consideration to the complications and needs their leaders had. The result is a generation of leaders who often feel isolated, recognizing the huge communication gap that we now have. Leaders don't feel they can rely on their members, members don't understand what leadership entails, and leaders don't have the support of other leaders outside their immediate ministries.

There are many reasons why we need to start to change how we approach spiritual fellowship for leaders. I believe we don't discuss it much now because most aren't sure how to solve the issue. Our vain attempts failed, and now leaders often feel like their problems are internal rather than real leadership needs and issues that must be discussed.

As a leader, what once worked for you as a lay member is not going to work for you as a leader. In most instances, church services and experiences are not designed for leaders. They are designed for lay members and visitors, individuals who are not in active ministry. The focus of the average church service, conference, or event is designed to help the average member in a church remain encouraged, focused, and dedicated to the Christian life. For example, when you select a sermon topic, conference theme, or event schedule, you keep in mind your congregation's needs. It's not something you want to hear about or something that will help you grow, but something that will help them develop their spiritual lives. This is part of leadership, but it can definitely leave a leader feeling void. As much as you might love leading your congregation or ministry, you probably get bored with the limitations you find in discussion, teaching, and preaching. It can feel like you are talking about the same things all the time, and that's probably because on some level, you are.

On this same level, one of the reasons why the throngs of leadership networks failed is because the leaders of those networks treated the leaders they led like they were congregants. Topics, themes, and ideas for teaching were often more emphatic versions of what they taught their laity, thus failing to meet the needs those in leadership had. It's not uncommon to see leaders leading other leaders who shouldn't, because they don't understand the unique needs other leaders have when in ministry. It's perfectly possible to be great with laity and not with other leaders – but this is definitely a topic for another time. The point is it's easy for leaders to get lost in the shuffle, not finding teaching that challenges them or meets their needs as they lack the fellowship and spiritual guidance to discover more of what they need.

Leaders are no better than laity before God, but being a leader is different than being a lay member of a church. Leaders face different levels of expectation and responsibility. They do not just face the challenges of Christian living, but those challenges along with those of leadership. Leaders spend much of their time attending to the needs of others and addressing those needs. If you do that long enough without any spiritual inspiration, you come up dry.

How do we handle this problem?

The first thing we need to understand are the spiritual needs of leaders. We will start by saying leaders are often interested in exploring and studying Scripture on a different level than the average lay member. While lay members read the Bible to find encouragement and answers to life's problems, leaders Scripture more intensely. They desire to know more about the ins and outs of spiritual things and seek to know the Scriptures in more than an everyday life approach to problems. They want to see God in the situations of old, recognize the depths of truth present in the Scriptures, understand language and culture present in Scripture, and discuss the Scriptures in a deep, educational way. While we can always find a refresher course in everyday life application, leaders should desire to see results from living their lives in the Spirit and applying the truths of Scripture. Rather than be reminded of things, most leaders want to learn more about the Scriptures than can be accomplished in a

Sunday morning sermon, a Wednesday night Bible study, or an occasional conference.

Second, leaders should strive to be better educated in matters of faith than lay members. If for no other reason, they should seek this goal to be effective leaders. Some of the finer points of faith – accuracy of doctrine, discerning what is within others, making sure things are done decently and in order – means leaders must educate themselves on spiritual and procedural matters. If a leader is educating themselves or has educated themselves (with the understanding that continued education is necessary, of course), this is going to radically shift how they view things others don't consider much. Whereas a lay member might be perfectly comfortable in a spiritual setting with a great amount of disorder behind-the-scenes, a leader may take issue in that situation.

Third, a leader has a different relationship with their leaders than a lay member has with their leader. Yes, some things in leadership are universal, but a leader who handles other leaders (such as an apostle or a prophet) is going to interact differently with those they lead as opposed to a leader who works with laity. Leaders led by other leaders (within God's order) may not have their leader at their disposal because they might live in another city or take care of many other leaders at the same time. The relationship is more instructional (training) and discussion (counseling and encouragement) and they help the leader develop and grow their ministry, usually through a discussion and connection process. This is different from laity who see their leader regularly, experience the benefits of their leader's presence, and receive additional help, such as counseling or guidance, whenever it is needed.

Fourth, leaders often don't have many immediate friends or family around them to help when they go through an issue.

Part of being a leader means you are just that – a leader – and not everyone around you is able to pour in or stimulate the mind or faith like someone on the same level is able to do so. Most leaders also shoulder the burden of households, families, children, and secular jobs. They aren't expected to need a break or reprieve from the complications of ministry combined with everyday life. It can also be difficult for leaders to deal with the pressure to "keep up appearances." It seems like as long as a minister's family resembles something seen on a Christmas card, everyone refrains from judgment. This leads to dishonesty, the feeling that when things are less than perfect or when a leader needs help and support the most, they can't reach out.

The solutions to these issues are complicated, but they aren't impossible to overcome. We need to start with a few key things, all of which will take a little time to implement. If we start with one or two good habits at a time, we can move in a much better direction than where the church stands right now.

- **Expect something of our laity** – It's a wonderful idea to think leaders can always rely on other leaders to get through problems. It's also an unrealistic one. If we look at the New Testament, it's unreasonable to think the early church apostles always had other leaders around to encourage them. They were forging new territory, doing something new, and sometimes (especially based on the letters we have in the New Testament) they were on their own, trying to teach and lead the church by themselves. Leaders are still part of the Body of Christ, and it's important we see ourselves that way, even if other leaders are nowhere to be found. Laity needs to understand the work of leadership, especially in the context of identity and responsibility. They need to learn about praying for and supporting their leader, about the importance of being there and being able to interact with their leader, and recognizing leadership is human, with human frailties and complications. Just as leaders need to be good leaders, laity needs to be good members: participating in church, loving their leader, giving cheerfully, and supporting their leader in good times and bad. The church takes all of us, and leaders need to be able to rely on their membership as much as anyone else.

- **Develop a good relationship with your own leader** – Given what I discussed earlier in this section, it's difficult to find a good leader who is equipped to lead other leaders. Sometimes we, as leaders, forget why good leaders are important for us and we settle for mediocre ones or we don't develop a good relationship with them in the process. It is imperative for leaders, especially those starting out, to have a solid relationship with their leader, no matter how far away or near your leader may be. Make some time to talk to them, share your thoughts, engage with their training, and most importantly, meet others who are a part of their ministry, brothers and sisters who are a part of your fellowship. Most likely, you have much in common with some of them, and that is why you have been drawn to your leader, at this time, in your ministry. If you are a leader, you need to be sitting under an apostle (apostles, prophets, evangelists, pastors, teachers, and the appointments) or under a prophet (prophets).

- **Participating in your leader's ministry as a member** – All of us need to have a place where we are a follower, and not a leader. While yes, we still need to be connected to a ministry that leads with leaders in mind, we also need to relieve ourselves of the burden of having to lead something else all the time. It's pragmatic, practical advice that reminds us of our need to continue in spiritual disciplines that are universal to all believers. As leaders, we do this in environments designed to meet our greater leadership needs while providing stability and humility to help ground us as people. It is an important – and essential – balancing act that is accomplished well as we grow with and through our leaders and our ministry experiences.

- **Personal devotion** – Every believer needs personal devotional time. Leaders often skip their devotional time in favor of trying to get a head start on ministry tasks. Skipping devotional time is a bad habit that, if you are regularly doing, you need to stop. Leaders need that intense, consistent, personal connection to God to continue to guide effectively. If we stop seeking Him, we cease to hear His voice. Devotional time doesn't have to mean it takes on a stereotypical or standard character of reading three-and-a-half chapters of the Bible every day and sitting with a prayer book or hymnal in hand. Sometimes devotional time may mean just being quiet with God, sometimes exploring unknown Biblical territory, sometimes lying in His presence, sometimes listening to worship music, and sometimes doing some intense praying. Whatever your personal devotional time is, find that niche of personal devotion, and make sure you don't skip out on it for anything.

- **Seminary/academics** – Sometimes we ignore the educational and scholarly aspects of ministry, thinking these things can't be spiritual. The truth is that yes, while seminary is an experience of ministry engagement and training, it is also an important outlet for the intellectual side of ministry often lacking in modern-day ministry settings. In ministry, we tend to deal with many people who have specific concepts about what a church leader should be. We spend much of our time handling personalities, conflicts, and trying to reach individuals with fundamental principles, over and over again. If you have a true love of Scripture, seminary and Bible training can be an important door opening to academic discussion and understanding of Scripture on a different level than is often handled within our churches. It can also offer us different perspectives about ministry, including opportunities to teach, network, or fellowship with people of faith and belief outside of church.

- **Developing bonds with other leaders** – Those leaders who have been hurt or wounded by other leaders tend to have difficulty trusting leaders as friends. This is completely understandable, as the average ministry situation is quite cutthroat. It can feel like everyone is out to destroy or harm a minister's work or calling, and that can lead to a severe sense of isolation. It doesn't help that some leaders act without proper etiquette or conduct, and that can also lead a leader to bow out of many social situations where they might otherwise connect and meet leaders who have similar struggles.

I am not saying a leader should be a part of messy or unseemly associations, or that you should compromise your own principles to be accepted or liked by other ministers. What I am saying is ministers should always recognize the importance in having friends around them, especially those that are able to understand what they go through as ministers of the Gospel. Whether it comes in the form of a leader's support group or it is found in great friends who serve as mutual counsel and support, such is essential for ministry success.

As a leader, it's all right to have your ups and downs. Hopefully, by following some of the advice given in this section, you will be able to manage some of the downs a little better. By finding what you need, you will become an even better minister.

How do I get others outside of my family interested in my ministry?

Most ministries start out with a following of immediate family and close friends. There are a few reasons for this, probably the most important being family and friends know the minister doing the work, they are interested because they know that person, they have a sense of them as an individual and want to be supportive. Their sense of obligation to help may or may not be out of a true understanding of the work you are doing or of being there led by the Holy Spirit, but they are there because, most likely, they want to be there for you. This is motivated by a well-intentioned spirit, and it can lead to great and wonderful things in your relationship with these people, not to mention their relationship with God. If they are open to what He wants to do, they can experience the blessing and bounty of what He is doing in your ministry, and that can turn into a powerful opportunity for them, too.

Sometimes those closest to us may show up for reasons that aren't so good. There are those occasions where people show up to be difficult or with the expectation of your failure. When it comes to these situations, discernment is key in handling them. Sometimes we need to ask people to leave or give them that option, making it clear we are doing this work for the Lord, not so others can watch us fail. It's important to remember this isn't always the situation, so seeking God and talking to a trusted leader are key when such is the situation.

There's nothing wrong, nor to be ashamed of, if you have a ministry full of supportive family and friends. The only time it becomes a problem is when somewhere down the line ten years later, that's all who is there. When churches and ministries are familial controlled for so long, others get the message you really don't want anyone else in your group. This doesn't happen right away, and it's best to erase these long-term thoughts from your mind. The best thing to do to grow your church is mobilize evangelism among your own. I would recommend some study and teaching on the issues in your neighborhoods and communities. Provide outreach talking points and projects for your group to let others know you are there. Encourage family and friends to bring a guest to service or study with them. As you reach out wider, you will start to see, little by little, that you will have more people in your ministry or church than just relatives. If your family and friends start to taper off as you grow, that is to be expected. Recognize their season with this work is up. If they remain, then you can know the Spirit has moved in and through them, and they are here because God has called them to this work.

My spouse is not interested in being in ministry or supporting me in ministry... so what happens now?

In New Testament times, Christianity disrupted relationships in a far more obvious way than we see today. While dedication to Christian faith (in all its forms) might cause internal discord or dissention today, it's nothing like in the early days of Christianity. Devotion to the faith caused notable political and social discord, so much so that spouses had each other killed, they might have had their children or other family members killed, people publicly defamed or martyred, and believers paid a huge price for bearing the Name of Christ. They experienced more than private discord or strain on a marriage; they paid through violence with their lives.

Why do I mention this? Even though their service to the Lord came at a high and intense price, they continued to serve the Lord. If it was a choice between their lives and their faith, there was no question their lives would be the thing to go. The level of faith these believers had and the intensity of their devotion and commitment to the call of Christ is overwhelming. It also makes the reasons we often avoid ministry sound very small. I don't mean to suggest the dilemma you are facing is of no consequence, because it certainly is. But the question as to whether you should do ministry if your spouse is uninterested in it or in supporting it shouldn't be a thought. If God has called you to do ministry, then He knows your circumstances and has equipped you to handle whatever comes along in the journey to ministry fulfillment.

We love the idea of content, passionate ministers with dedicated spouses. The picture-perfect postcard family, complete with a loving spouse and obedient children, permeates our concepts and ideas of ministry life. We don't consider ministry requires a lot of the spouse, equally if not as much as it does the minister. While the expectations are different, ministry spouses must consider time factors, sharing their spouse with the ministry, emergencies and interruptions, accusations, and other complications that make ministry life a part of their regular existence. Not every spouse is interested in the way ministry can overtake life, and maybe understandably so, isn't enthusiastic at the idea of their life partner pursuing something that will take them away from their marriage. There are a few things to consider when discussing marriage and ministry, especially when you have a spouse that is unsupportive.

The first posture we take in life is as a Christian and God's servant. This posture comes before spouse, parent, child, and friend. No matter what we are called to do in this life or with who we associate, we belong to God and must obey God. If God has told you to be in ministry, obeying that is paramount to your life. It is part of your relationship with Him and that relationship must come first – before anyone and anything else – in your life. This isn't to say that you don't have existing responsibilities, or you should forsake your marriage or family. You don't get to have an "I'm doing this now, so everyone just get used to it!" attitude. It is understood that obeying God, especially with something as big as ministry, may cause conflict and disruption in a household situation, and everyone needs time to adjust to what God is doing in and through you. It does mean if you believe God has called you to do it, you must do it, whether your spouse is interested or not.

Likewise, there is nothing in Scripture that states a spouse must take interest in a ministry. Spouses represent a separate institution from church authority, and there is a clear distinction between the two. Just because someone is uninterested in ministry doesn't disqualify someone else from pursuing it.

This isn't to suggest you should abandon your marriage, nor does it mean it doesn't sting when your spouse turns their back on what God has called you to do. You are in the complicated situation of maintaining your marriage and your ministry. If ministry is what you are called to do, you must figure out a way to walk the line between the two. You aren't going to do it perfectly. Setting boundaries – both in your marriage and ministry – will be essential. I'd recommend having a conversation with your spouse about things and hearing how they are feeling. Yes, ministry means change; it also means you will better discover things about yourself, and by so doing, you will be better for your marriage, as well.

It is possible to maintain a marriage and also maintain a ministry, even if your spouse isn't interested. There's no way to predict the future, but there are definite steps you can take to move forward with the work God has called you to do. Yes, you must obey God, even in the face of spousal disapproval. Yes, you can still maintain your relationship and do your best to remain a committed, devoted spouse, even if they disagree with your decision. Just as you have prayed and God led you to ministry, so He will reveal how to handle this aspect of life for you, too.

My ministry doesn't seem to be going anywhere. Should I give up and pursue something else?

My first question is: what does "doesn't seem to be going anywhere" mean? How are you defining the current state of your ministry? This might sound like an odd response to your question but bear with me for a minute. Whenever we start feeling like we aren't "going anywhere," it is usually because we define our ministry according to the success we assume others have. We look around and see bigger ministries, ministries with more money and more notoriety, and we don't think we are "going anywhere."

At some point we have all succumbed to the charms of "Christian Hollywood," mega-church preachers and groups that seem to have it all: money, popularity, and plenty of defenders, even in the face of spiritual realities that are less than accurate. No matter the scandal or bad press, people still flock to their services, buy their books, and love these preachers. It can make even the most dedicated person question what they are doing and think there is something they are missing.

There's an old expression I once heard: Whenever a foot measures itself against a yard, it always comes up short. There is nothing better about being a yard than a foot; they are just different units of measurement. Each one has its purpose, and if a foot travels three times its own length, it'll be the same distance as a yard (even though it remains a foot). The same is true about ministry. When you are called to ministry, your calling is unique. It's not like nor the same as someone else's. We are not called to do the same things or look the same in our work. It is our differences that ensure every area of Kingdom need is covered. The focus you have must reflect what God wants you to do as you develop your work. The pace you move at, the flow of your work, its size, and its scope are unique to you.

This means your concept of ministry success must be reevaluated to follow the standard God has established, not the standard others follow. None of us know what God has instructed someone else to do. It is possible to have all the success we deem relevant in this world and be completely out of God's will for ministry. Instead of looking at what others are doing, we need to see if we are obedient to what God has told us to do. If you do what God instructs, you will find your success and satisfaction in that, whether it looks like what someone else is doing, or not.

I highly doubt your ministry isn't "going anywhere." It just doesn't look like what someone else is doing. Take your eyes off of their work and focus on God's instruction and direction for you. There you will find the next steps you are supposed to take, and exactly where those steps are to take you for the work of the Lord.

I DON'T WANT TO SLIGHT MY CHILDREN BY BEING IN MINISTRY, BUT I KNOW I CAN'T DO AS MUCH FOR THEM AS I DO NOW IF I PURSUE IT. WHAT SHOULD I DO?

We like to talk about the benefits and blessings of ministry, and both do come along with it. Yet there is the often unspoken, not-so-secret aspect of ministry we don't talk about: sacrifice. We know sacrifice is part of ministry; we know sacrifice exists in ministry; but we don't ever dare to talk about why it's there or how to handle it, especially in family situations. This has made ministerial sacrifice a taboo subject and leaves many ministers unprepared in how to handle it when its necessity arises.

When we take on the work of ministry, we take on the ministry of Christ. This doesn't mean we become Christ Himself, but it does mean we experience some of what He experienced. One of these things is sacrifice, or having to choose between one thing and another, giving something up in the process. Sometimes we will be forced to choose between ministry and something else, maybe even something we might want or want to do. For example, people who are financially irresponsible are unsuccessful in ministry. If you want to be in ministry, that may mean not spending so much money, cutting up credit cards, or not getting a new car or house. This is one of the prime ways ministry impacts those who have families in a different way from those who are single. When these decisions must be made, it affects the family as well as the minister. For you to do what God has called you to do, everyone must make certain concessions and live with the necessary sacrifices.

I've often said we hear the lie in church that we should "have it all:" the spouse, the big house, the children, the job, the ministry, the social life, the perfect presentation. The truth behind this lie is we can't have it all, at least not all at once. To have it all requires money, time, and effort. When it comes down to the realities of ministry, we can't do all those things at once and expect any of them to come out successfully. In life, we must make choices. That means if we have young children, someone must take care of them, and focus on that, during that time of their lives. If we want a big house, a big house costs money, and we need to help pay for that. If we want a social life and the perfect image, there's a lot of things that come along with such that cost us somewhere else. When it comes to ministry, if we want to be in ministry, other things must be sacrificed so we can have the startup funds, the focus, and the attention for what we are supposed to do.

I understand you want to do the best for your kids (and that as of asking this question, your children are no longer babies, requiring full-time care), but sometimes our concept of what's best is not what is truly best for everyone. If you are called to be in ministry and it means you won't be able to buy your kids all the latest devices or trendy things, it means maybe there is something for them to learn in not getting so many things from you all the time. There are lots of other ways kids can be loved and appreciated, and it means that yes, maybe all the "new" stuff is off the table for a little while, but there are many ways and many things you can do for your kids that don't cost money.

If spending time with your kids is of concern, there is no reason why you can't spend time with your kids, even if you are in ministry. Having a mom who is in ministry teaches kids about priorities, and while there may be times when you have to go and do things instead of being with them, that is not the case, all the time. It is great for kids to come along and see you minister if that is an option, and to have them pitch in and help around the house in your absence.

What you should do is obey God and trust Him for the rest. This doesn't mean becoming a neglectful parent. You just need to discover your new normal and find your balance while you answer His call. I have no question whether you will figure it out. No, you won't always do things perfectly, but you will find your purpose, and in the process, stand as an example for your children in following the will of God and the sacrifice that sometimes comes along with it.

I AM A SINGLE MINISTER. I WANT TO BE MARRIED, BUT I DON'T SEEM TO MEET ANYONE RIGHT FOR ME. WHY IS THIS?

I am excited to know you are a minister and have discovered this about yourself at this point in your life. Some people have a hard time hearing from God when they are lonely or unhappy, and it can make it much harder to do ministry. As a fellow minister who discovered her calling when single and who had to readjust to single life after my husband died, I laud you for moving forward despite the challenges and difficulties you face as a single minister. It takes a lot to keep going when things are hard. For your perseverance, you should celebrate.

As for your personal situation, I am sorry you find the world of dating (with the goal of marriage) so challenging. I know how you feel; I deal with the same challenges now in my life, and it's not easier because I am now older. You are not alone; the truth is most people find dating to be a difficult process, especially after we know dating isn't what we desire long-term. It becomes even more frustrating and complicated when we don't seem to be able to connect with the right person for our desired relationship. It's unfortunate, but I don't feel church folks often help in the situation. Much of the advice we get sounds a lot like victim shaming – somehow your single state is your fault. You're told you aren't exercising enough faith, or you are too "churchy," or somehow you are chasing a "type" that isn't for you. Some go the other way and say you aren't praying or prepared enough! Instead of encouraging you, the advice they give keeps you busy but makes you feel inadequate within yourself, all at the same time.

It's my understanding that is exactly what the advice is designed to do – keep you busy but not offer you any sustainable answers. That's probably because no one has a real answer as to why you haven't met anyone who is right for you. They want you to stay busy and focused on the things of God. They do not want you to stray into areas of temptation or abandon the things of God. No matter how well-intentioned they may be, they do not realize in telling you the things they do, their words cause you to feel even more lonely. This isn't how God wants you to feel, and it is certainly an understandable frustration to feel ready for something new in your life that doesn't seem to come.

The first thing I would say is there may very well be nothing you are doing to keep you from meeting someone. Dating can be a confusing navigational pool, especially with the advance of online dating. People aren't always upfront about what they want, hesitation to meet people in person is a thing, and some have confusing or conflicting views about relationships and their expectations therein. How people engage in relationships can be complicated, as we are all influenced by several factors: age, general upbringing, spiritual upbringing, educational level, and current spiritual affiliation. Whenever you are approaching a possible relationship, many of these underlying issues aren't stated up front, but come out later. It can be frustrating to realize some things are there that perhaps you wish were not.

Dating can be a very confusing experience, especially for a minister who seeks a responsible, mature partner in life. The best thing you can do is be clear about your own ideas and values; open to meeting new people and seeing where things go; know what is important to you as a person; and what you are seeking in a mate. It might seem like this quickly eliminates many potential dates, but if they aren't right for you, they aren't a potential mate.

This is essential to understanding and knowing yourself in the dating process. When we date someone, we don't just learn about them; we also learn about ourselves. We learn what we want and don't want, what we seek, what we enjoy, and how we can best be honest in every situation.

There is also the possibility that, in being honest with yourself, you might discover other things that are keeping you, at this time, from meeting someone who is right for you. Are you too busy for a relationship? Ministry tends to keep us very busy, especially if a ministry is new or growing. As a minister, you often have to do much of the work yourself. Sometimes we don't meet anyone because we aren't accessible (in time or location). If this is the case, you must figure out a solution. How can you make more time for yourself? Do you need some new hobbies or some additional leisure time? Another possibility is that in the pursuit of being married, you need to expand the idea of meeting different people. Ministers can be a closed vault of emotional mire, and this means we put our best foot forward, reserving part – or all – of who we might be behind our Sunday smiles. Along these same lines, we sometimes get so caught up in our concept of who and what we want (expecting that same best foot forward for potential mates) we ignore good possibilities who don't fit the ideals we established. Balance is crucial in all things, especially as we realize no potential mate – even the best possible choice for us – is perfect. Introduce some variety into your life: take a class, explore a hobby, do something that gets you out of where you are – so you can meet and experience different kinds of people.

In all things, use wisdom: Avoid international scams when dating online, use good judgment about your mate, and never appear desperate. If a situation doesn't feel right to you, it probably isn't, so do not pursue it. Above all, do know God hears your heart, and examining where you are and what you want is the best way to finding a better sense of contentment while you continue to seek a mate who is ready – and right – for you.

As a Minister, What Should I Look For in a Mate?

You cannot know how overjoyed I am to see you have asked this question. As a single minister, I know you face immense pressure to marry someone, and it seems like everyone has an opinion over what "type" or what person is "right for you." At some point in time, you must do something very important for yourself: you need to shut them all out and focus on God, on what you need as a person, and what you need in a spouse as a minister of the Lord.

There are a few things to consider about any potential mate when you are a minister. Just like being married to a lawyer, an EMT, or doctor brings certain expectations, being married to a minister requires certain things of the individual you marry. Believe it or not, you have a huge edge over those who married before they were in ministry: you are able to consider the specific needs you have as a minister and have time to think about what you need in a mate.

First thing: why do you want to be married? This may seem like a strange question, but there are many reasons why someone may want to be married…and the reasons aren't always good. If you feel like you must get married because others are pressuring you, getting married will prove disastrous. If you know why you want to marry it makes it easier to know what you seek in a mate.

Second, you need to consider what characteristics you seek in someone. This is something every single person seeking a relationship should do, but it is more relevant when you are a minister. Do you want someone who can take charge at home, especially in your absence? Do you want to have an equal say in everything that happens? Are you good at personal care and self-management, or do you need help with those things? How involved do you want to be in your home life? Do you want a mate who is a good listener, good talker, or all right with silence? What kind of companionship do you need?

Third, how involved do you want your mate to be in your ministry? If the answer is you don't want someone involved, there's nothing wrong with this, just as there's nothing wrong if you want them involved. It's important consider their own desires on the topic, so a conversation will be necessary. Even if your mate is not involved, they will need to understand navigating the different situations that come along with being the partner of a minister.

In looking over these three big things you will, most likely, come up against many smaller things; that's all right, it is what this process is for. You probably also have other points of interest that are important to you as a person. Those should be considered as much as any other point in this process. In all things, pray about it. Consider all areas of a person, their personality, and their interests, to select a mate that is worthy of you and of partnering with you in life as you pursue ministry.

I AM A MINISTER AND EVERYONE WANTS ME TO GET MARRIED. THEY SAY IT WILL "BETTER MY MINISTRY." WHAT IS WRONG WITH MY MINISTRY NOW?

I don't personally know of your ministry, but I can say from experience there is probably nothing wrong with your ministry now, at least not on the level you are thinking. You're experiencing the sting of perspective, and it has nothing to do with you personally, as a minister. The problem is it certainly feels that way. It feels like you are the odd minister out: the one everyone questions, the one who isn't invited to preach at events unless they are specifically for singles, and the one no one feels is qualified to counsel others. You wind up excluded from fancy events and picked at with incessant questions, all because you are not married.

One thing that bothered me most in my ministry history was the way people changed toward me after I got married the first time. My message, style, and ministry were exactly the same as before, but people treated me differently. Whereas no one would give me the time of day earlier, now I was seen as relevant. Someone else might have been thrilled that people were taking notice, but I was angry. It made me feel like I wasn't assessed on my merit, but on some external thing that in the long run, wasn't a very good experience for me.

People responded to me differently after I got married because they identified with me. People like to identify with their teachers, leaders, and spiritual mentors. Judgments tend to be made based on what they recognize in someone's humanity versus being led by the Spirit. They like to think their leaders can personally relate to whatever they're going through. This is the reason why many say that an unmarried minister (regardless of gender) is unqualified to do couples' counseling and should never talk about marriage. If you haven't done it or been through it yourself, it's assumed you can't possibly know what it's like to experience it. Being married is seen as a sign of maturity, of experiencing life's sacrifice and being a true adult, whereas being single is seen as being commitment-phobic, self-centered, and immature. These are merely stereotypes and not realities, but it is amazing how many people buy into this logic, disguising it under spiritual feelings or advice, generation after generation.

People think your ministry will be "bettered" by marriage because you will then have the experience of being married. There are many who equate marriage to some sort of spiritual enlightenment or experience. This is the opposite of what many felt and thought in earlier church times. It was often expected ministers would prefer single life when in ministry; running a household and having a family was seen as conflicting with spiritual things. It doesn't have to be a conflict, but at the same time, it doesn't mean everyone has to get married, either. We know Jesus never married, nor did the Apostle Paul. We take the marital advice from two unmarried individuals, upholding them as inspired reflections of the Word of God. This means it is possible to have a perfectly fine ministry as a single person, it is perfectly possible for God to speak through a single person as pertains to marital and relationship advice, and that no human being can experience all of human experience, so our standards in this regard must quickly change.

Marriage is not for everyone. It's perfectly possible to serve in ministry as a single person, whether for a season or permanently. It's also important to say that we should never get married with the hope or intention of furthering or developing our ministries. I laud you for not running into it head-first, thinking it will give you social positioning in your life. I am also very sorry you feel your ministry is being diminished by others. I pray you will be led to those who will value your ministry regardless of your marital status. There are people ready to receive a great spiritual word, and I pray your ministry will attract those who recognize God can use any vessel He desires to preach His Word.

I'M A SINGLE MOTHER. CAN I STILL BE IN MINISTRY?

If we look at the Scriptures, there are many examples of single mothers we often ignore. Because the woman is described as a "widow" or a "concubine," we don't think of her as a single mother...but that is exactly what she was. In ancient times, there wasn't much difference between a widow or a concubine and a mother whose child was born out of wedlock, with one difference: a widow with a male child had assurance familial property would remain in the family (if there was any), as long as there were no outstanding debts or other reason why the property had to be sold, transferred, or deferred. Sometimes the latter did happen, and many widows without a male relative to care for them found themselves destitute. This also happened when a husband was unable to provide for his family and did not have property or land rights from the start. Such would have left a woman alone, forced to take care of her child or children and herself.

Single parenting is not new. Throughout history, women have been single parents from pregnancy outside of marriage, prostitution, the death of a spouse, famine, war, violence, poverty, divorce, and other aspects of life that changed and challenged a woman's immediate situation. Because women were regarded as caretakers, it was understood that no matter a circumstance, women would care for children (no matter how laborious or impossible it might become). Much like today, single mothers bore the burden of caring for children alone while struggling to also care for themselves.

There have been single mothers in ministry throughout history. It can be difficult to balance both, and how you decide to handle single parenting and ministry work is your own call. Some women decide to wait until their child is a certain age or out of the house to pursue ministry, some decide to move forward regardless of the situations. No matter what your choice, you will be the one to discern your own balancing act between parenthood and ministry.

If you are pursuing the things of God, handling parenthood to the best of your ability, and you know and desire to do more in ministry, than by all means, follow God's leading. Don't let being a single parent stop you. By being a single parent and raising a child well and in the faith, you are already a success story.

How Do I Balance Ministry Money and Personal Finances?

If your ministry requires a personal financial commitment, you are not alone. The majority of new ministers must start with at least a small financial investment. At some point in time, the balance of personal and ministry finances usually works itself out, without the minister having to take their own money to invest in the work. The question is, how do you balance the needs of ministry with your own personal financial needs? The answer is simpler than you might imagine.

The simple answer: save a little, spend a little, give a little. These are the principles of budgeting: make sure your expenses are covered and then have some to spend, some to save, and some to give.

Whether in ministry or not, every one of us should have a household budget to assess our financial needs. Budgets provide a regular inventory of how much money you have coming in and how much money you have going out. When we budget, we can see our financial realities: owed bills, expenses, and income, all in a way that helps us figure out how much we can give to our ministry startup. We should have some money that is saved, some that is spent, and some that is given. Money for a ministry would classify as money spent and may come from some that is saved, because those are generated after we cover necessary expenses. Just how much you spend is your choice, but most recommend operating by a tithe principle: ten percent to give, ten percent to spend, and ten percent to save, with the existing seventy percent for bills and expenses. Obviously, there are months where this doesn't always work out the way you might hope, but as a good rule, this stands for purpose and is the general advice given to people when it comes to budgeting.

There are some other general guidelines to follow when it comes to ministry finances and sorting out the often-difficult road of ministry money. These are:

- **Never use ministry money for household problems or emergencies** – It's fine for you to contribute to your ministry, but it is neither legal nor right for you to take ministry money for yourself. Doing so will make it difficult for you to maintain non-profit status and will lend you a terrible reputation.

- **Do not use ministry status to recruit funds for personal situations** – It's not everyone else's fault you can't cover your apartment's rent, you must move, you need a new car, you are short on your bills one month, or you have difficulty maintaining your own finances. Asking others to cover your expenses is not just begging, it also sends the message you can't handle money. This makes people leery about giving and causes them to look on you negatively.

- **Sort out debt and credit issues** – It's simple enough to say everyone has bad credit and extensive debt, but this isn't true. When we are in ministry, credit is everything as we work to create a reputable, professional name for ourselves. Since we are the ones people often check out, it is essential we resolve credit and debt issues. It may take some time, but in the long run, it will be well worth it.

Always remember ministries are not built in a day. When it comes to ministry finances, not all ministry problems can be solved by obtaining larger sums of money. It's easy for us to fall into the trap of comparison and look around, seeing other ministers in different situations than we are in, automatically assuming if we had more money we could be where they are. You are called to do a unique work, it takes time to build, and as you establish fiscal responsibility, you will see transformation and elevation in your ministry. Just remember, don't spend more than you can on your ministry, and always keep in mind the basic principle of saving a little, spending a little, and giving a little.

WHAT DOES IT MEAN WHEN PEOPLE TELL ME MY HOME IS MY FIRST MINISTRY?

This phrase (and its sentiments) is invoked with one agenda, and one agenda alone: to make ministers feel guilty, as if their work in ministry causes them to neglect their families. By saying "your home is your first ministry," someone is letting you know they disapprove of something you're doing and are being critical of a situation they probably know nothing about.

Let's get this out of the way: there are ministers out there who use ministry to avoid responsibilities at home. Some do pursue ministry to the neglect of their spouses and children. Some of the biggest names in ministry were and are rather neglectful as spouses and parents because the demands of their ministries required them to be away from home for long periods of time. We laud the spouses of such ministers, but many of them were and are, in many ways, single parents.

I will never deny that ministry is demanding, and these demands occupy much of our lives. I will also say most ministers I know aren't trying to avoid their responsibilities at home. If anything, I meet many ministers who use their life responsibilities as an excuse to avoid pursuing the call of ministry! Most ministers are trying to navigate the very difficult and challenging waters of balancing home and family, personal and ministry identity, and taking care of their families while pursuing what they know God has called them to do.

It should also be said there is nothing anywhere in Scripture that states a minister's home is her "first ministry." There is nothing in the Bible that defines marriage or family as "ministry." They may be opportunities for service and for the opportunity to minister to one another through that life venue, and it, most likely, will bring about a certain level of spiritual revelation and personal insight. This is different, however, from standing as a minister in a leadership capacity over a church or ministry, and it is important we grow in our understanding to distinguish between the two. Merging them all the time means we don't recognize what is appropriate where, and we don't know how to best govern our personal lives along with our professional work in God's Kingdom.

When someone tells you, "your first ministry is at home," politely inform them you have your house and your ministry both under control. You do not need their advice or perspectives on personal governance. If they persist, you have every right to walk away, hang up the phone, and discontinue the discussion. Whether in ministry or not, some things are just not other people's business. We would have a much better time in church if people would attend to their own issues and live out their own philosophies as opposed to imposing those on others.

ALL THE MEN I DATE SEEM INTERESTED IN "DOING MINISTRY TOGETHER" OR MERGING MINISTRY, USUALLY BY HIM TAKING CONTROL OF THE WORK. I AM NOT COMFORTABLE WITH THIS. WHAT DO YOU SAY?

As of the writing of this book, I have been in ministry well over two decades. I have done ministry single, partnered, married, estranged, widowed, dating, and beyond – and the major problem I had in most personal relationships I pursued was this very issue. Whether they had a ministry or not, it seemed like every single time things would seem promising, someone would drop the bomb that signaled the end: they would want to do ministry "together." The problem with "together" is it usually meant he thought he should take over and I should welcome that, even though I had more experience and…well…it was my ministry!

You should never, ever be comfortable with someone coming along and taking control, authority, or position in your ministry by proxy. When someone feels they have an entitlement to your ministerial work because they know you personally, they need to be corrected. We wouldn't tolerate this from someone we lead in our ministry. We wouldn't tolerate this from our friends. We wouldn't tolerate it from outside sources. Most of us probably wouldn't even tolerate it from family members. So why do we even hesitate to think we should tolerate it from those we know in a personal context?

The reason women even begin to entertain this idea is because of what we are told about relationships in church. Nine times out of ten, we hear that men are leaders and they always, whether right or wrong, "have rule" over us. We accept this in our personal lives as well as our ministries. Somehow, some way, without even considering the ramifications, we think allowing someone else to come in and take over our work is for our benefit. It's not, and we could describe this as is a classic case of "usurping authority." When someone usurps authority, it means they take an authority they do not have. It can be a perceived authority, a desired authority, or a conceptual authority, but the point is that it's not someone else's to have. To come into a ministry that is not your own and take it over by virtue of gender, relationship, or anything else is a classic definition of usurping authority. According to the Scriptures, it is something that should not be allowed in any ministry.

Men are not qualified to lead ministries simply because they are men, period. They are certainly not qualified to come in and take over an existing ministry because the leader therein is female. If a man did this to another man, there would be no end to the criticism and question as to the character of the man who did it. Yet it is done to women all the time by men for personal reasons, and no one thinks twice about it. It can't be order when it's done to a woman and a lack thereof when it's done to a man. It must be all right all the time or never all right, and the answer is that it is never, ever all right for someone else to come in and assume position in ministry authority without permission, placement by the leader, and an appropriate discernment period.

When we are in ministry and we pursue a personal relationship, we must always consider the person we are dating considering our work as much as considering our personal selves. This may sound difficult or complicated, but our lives as ministers are not just about us and what we want. We don't have the convenience of keeping who we are involved with as a secret for very long, because others see us out and about and wonder what is going on. While there do need to be healthy boundaries between you and those you lead, who you are involved with reflects on your ministry, can impact the people you lead, can reflect on your authority, and can also speak about the kind of person you are.

I've been in ministry for many years and have spent those years establishing rapport and reputation for the work I do. The people who have come to me and have chosen my leadership have done so because I am their leader, and they feel called to connect with the anointing upon my life. It would be wrong for me to suddenly hand them off to someone else because I have chosen to be in a personal relationship. Callings are different, abilities are different, and thinking someone I know on a personal level is qualified to lead my own people and take authority over them – and over myself – is both unfair to them and spiritually wrong. Each ministry has its own unique spiritual expressions, and we must be willing to uphold those, no matter what might come against us.

The men you are involved with probably have received the same bad messages you have, but that means you have a couple of options. The first is to explain what I have discussed here with them and show them what they are doing is in error. They have every option to work in their own ministries or establish their own work, without taking yours over or expecting that your ministries will merge into one. You can always do some joint ministry projects or do some work together without usurping anyone's authority or expecting either one of you to forsake what you are doing. Another option is they can develop support for what you do, working in helps or other behind-the-scenes projects to continue the ministry and keep it going (if they do not have their own ministry). A third option is that they can pursue what they already do if it is not ministry related (such as business or something else) and continue to be who they are, while you continue to be who you are. As a minister in a relationship, your partner must come to an understanding of who you are as a minister and embrace that as part of who you are as a person. If they can't respect that aspect of your life, and the boundaries that go with that, then they are not the right person for you.

My Spouse is Unsaved and My Children are Wavering in Their Faith. Am I Qualified for Ministry?

I am glad you submitted this question because it's a controversial one. Depending on who you ask, you will receive different answers. The way we answer this question has to do with how we understand the Scriptures and the work of a minister, and we will take these issues, one at a time, to bring clarity to your situation.

It is true the Bible advises against marriage to non-believers, but that is not the beginning and the end of its position. There are exceptions to the standard, and the Bible gives advice about mixed marriage, especially in the New Testament. In the days of the early church, everyone was a convert to Christianity. As a result, not everyone was able to marry a believing spouse. The marital custom of that time was arranged marriage, not marriage by choice. Marriages were often planned between families in advance, and not all Christians had the convenience of marrying a believer. The apostle's words about light not having fellowship with darkness and about being unequally yoked were not about marriage but about mixing spiritual systems in worship. The concept of an unequal yoke extended to spiritual boundaries, the realities that sometimes we "fellowship" with people who are different from us and instead of upholding Christian values, we try to mix light and darkness. This is contrary to Christian witness, and that is a major reason why such was an issue in New Testament times. One could look at this example and automatically think it is all about mixed marriages, but that is not correct. I'm sure there were believers who dealt with intense pressure from marital strife and started mixing spiritual systems, following pagan ways to please their spouses while claiming Christian ways, but this was not a permanent reality, nor case. As many examples that seemed to downplay mixed marriage there are also many that upheld such, for spiritual reasons.

Mixed marriages didn't always lead to confusion. Gomer, Hosea's wife, was not spiritually right with God…and that is why God had Hosea choose her as a mate. Ruth, daughter-in-law of Naomi, was a Moabitess (a pagan), not a Jew. King Xerxes, who married Esther, was not a Jew and nowhere near the concept of salvation. These marriages served a purpose, and God was in every one of these situations, even though it seemed to contradict all the rules and guidelines that had been established. These marriages were necessary for many different reasons, and in keeping with that reality, they served God's purpose no matter how out of the ordinary they might have been.

I don't know what your specific situation is, but no matter what the case might be, you are married to your spouse, and it doesn't sound like you have any desire or intention to leave them. The Scriptures not only make allowances for such situations; they encourage such. 1 Corinthians 7:12-16 offers advice for this exact situation:

To the rest I say this (I, not the Lord): If any brother has a wife who is not a believer and she is willing to live with him, he must not divorce her. And if a woman has a husband who is not a believer and he is willing to live with her, she must not divorce him. For the unbelieving husband has been sanctified through his wife, and the unbelieving wife has been sanctified through her believing husband. Otherwise your children would be unclean, but as it is, they are holy.

But if the unbeliever leaves, let it be so. The brother or the sister is not bound in such circumstances; God has called us to live in peace. How do you know, wife, whether you will save your husband? Or, how do you know, husband, whether you will save your wife?

If you and your spouse are good with each other, you should stay together. If your spouse is in no way abusive, unfaithful, or problematic toward you, there is no reason why you should end your marriage over this issue. Instead of leaving an unbelieving spouse, your faith and life can stand as witness to them. If the two of you are working out your differences, then that's a testimony and a witness. Not every marriage ends in the conversion of the non-believing spouse, but that doesn't mean a marriage is unsuccessful. It just means that at this point in your marriage, you do not have a spouse who is a believer.

As for your children wavering in their faith, you haven't provided their ages, so I am assuming if they are old enough to waver in their faith they are at least in their teens, if not older. I think that children's and youth ministry are awesome things, but unfortunately, they aren't often done well enough to reach kids where they are, with the issues and thoughts they have about their faith in today's world. These programs are designed by adults who think they know (or imagine) what kids need, but they have no idea what kids are dealing with, experiencing, or feeling. As kids get older and it gets harder to answer their questions and keep them interested in spirituality, most parents feel unqualified to handle these matters and turn to these programs which also don't offer solutions. It's not an accident our churches are losing our children, and by the time they are young adults, we have often lost them, in one form or another, all together.

One thing often left out of youth ministry is a proper way

to handle the Scriptures as an adult. Throughout youth programs they skirt around issues related to youth, to try and get kids interested in the Bible. As they start to grow, they never introduce more advanced understanding of Bible matters to kids. I recommend talking to your children to discover where they are at and what issues they have with their faith. Talk to them as people. Encourage them to find answers to their questions, and find new, adult-like ways to start handling the Scriptures. Recognize what is present, and in trying to start dialogue, open the door for a new relationship with your children.

Different people have different assignments, and while some might disagree with me, I don't see your situation as a disqualification for ministry. If you have children at home behaving out of control or in a recklessly, you must consider how that will reflect on you, and that maybe it is in your best interest to try and handle those issues with your children before pursuing ministry on a larger scale. Overall, however, I feel that within your life and learning to sort out differences with your husband and find new points of encouragement with your children, you have an amazing testimony of endurance and consistency in the faith. It might not be the fairy-tale ending most expect, but it is the one that, in your ministry, will work for you.

I'M CONTEMPLATING A DIVORCE. HOW WILL THIS IMPACT MY MINISTRY?

I am sorry you find yourself in a situation that forces thoughts of divorce. I don't know what your circumstance is or why you are contemplating this move, but I can imagine if you are thinking about it, it isn't something you are doing with haste. I know how difficult divorce can be, especially for a minister, and that divorce is not something we take lightly. It's not a pleasant thing and can be very taxing emotionally, spiritually, and yes, even in the professional area of ministry. Considering all things and asking this question means you are doing everything right, and taking things in steps, which is probably the best advice I can give.

While I don't know your personal views as you consider matters of divorce, I will provide you a little bit of a backdrop on Biblical divorce to keep that from being a factor as you approach the situation. Divorce was sort of prohibitive in a Biblical sense (I'll explain more of what I mean by this in a minute) not for emotional or love reasons, but for the simple reason that marriage in ancient times was built upon different foundations than it is today. Because marriage was about alliances between families, tribes, clans, and nations, a divorce could upset whatever political and familial alliances were formed in that union. Instead of being allies, rivalries could form, which could easily lead to upsets between groups. This means marriage was about a lot more than just a couple and the issues that a couple might have faced. It was also about their immediate and extended families maintaining peace and keeping their agreements. Talk about a lot of pressure!

If we are going to be truly Biblical, however, divorce has never been entirely prohibitive, as some groups often teach. The Old Testament laws allowed a man to divorce a woman for any reason, and such was frequently invoked. It wasn't uncommon for a man to divorce a wife to take another in a tribal or familial arrangement (such as was the case with men marrying pagan women) and for men to, in the process, cause their wives and families to be destitute or sully the reputation of a woman because he didn't like her cooking. In the long run, this was not constructive, but it continued as cultural practices toward marriage also continued.

Fast-forward to New Testament times, Jesus was against divorce because it worked against the economic interests of women, children, and society as a nation. Women and children were seen as property, and the divorce laws were unjustly upheld in favor of male interests. When Jesus spoke on adultery as grounds for divorce, He only spoke in the context of men filing for divorce. Adultery was the focus due to ancient property rights. If a woman was with another man, that meant that man stole her husband's "property" and questions of paternity could arise. Adultery as a standard for divorce related to property, property rights, questions of inheritance and ultimately ownership, all to try and force the men of Israel to keep their commitments to their families.

Jesus' words were spoken within a specific context of marriage and divorce in a specific culture, neither of which are employed in most of the western world today. Marriages are no longer arranged, divorce laws demand certain equities and care for minor children, and a woman has the option to care for herself in the face of a divorce (although most divorce courts uphold certain provisions for care and property division that are far more equitable than in Biblical times). When we read Biblical statements about divorce and marriage, they weren't said regarding the laws and governances we have today. That's not to say we abandon everything in the text. Instead, we understand them in a better context, and we refrain from applying them in a narrow context of understanding. We recognize there are many different factors involved in marriage, and there are many reasons why people get divorced. Divorce is not something that anyone contemplates lightly. When it comes to divorce, we need to recognize there are many reasons why a couple may not be suitable to stay together (be it for emotional, spiritual, physical, or mental reasons). Since Jesus' statement about divorce was to encourage men to do right by their families, we can conclude if our marriage is harmful in any context, divorce is a legal and spiritual option.

How your divorce will impact your ministry relates to a few key things. The first is what level of authority you have in your ministry. For example: If you are a pastor with a church that has seen and knows your family, your spouse's absence will be notable to those around you. If you are an evangelist who preaches from time to time in a variety of different churches or someone who teaches in different locations, your spouse's presence might not be notable to begin with (especially if you travel alone all or most of the time). If you are an apostle, the level of impact will relate to whatever it is your spouse did in your ministry.

The next point relates to the last paragraph some; it also depends on how involved your spouse is with your ministry and how much you have mixed marriage and ministry. Many feel compelled to display their marriage, mention it in their biographies, and include their spouses in their work, sometimes to the point of positioning them in leadership. There are many reasons why I don't recommend the merger of marriage and ministry, and this is one of them. Whether or not we want to deal with it, relationships change; people get divorced, lose interest in ministerial work, people die, and life changes, all of which can impact a ministry if things are not properly handled. Divorce is one of those instances where ministry matters can get very messy. It is just easier, simpler, and more professional to handle ministry matters properly from the start. If that hasn't been the case, you will have the difficult task of explaining things to those under your ministry (without providing too many details and without being venomous or trying to make your spouse look bad), of deciding "who gets what" as far as items, property, and yes, possibly even people go (because there is the possibility if your spouse continues in ministry that some will desire to follow them), and the reality that people may change how they view the veracity of your ministry. If your marriage was used as a picture of God's will and purpose in your life and now it is over, that can easily cause people to question everything you teach, thus causing additional discord.

Divorce can also change your ministry image if people are familiar with your image as a married individual. Divorce is one of those issues the church does not agree about. Whether people's views on the issue are fair or not isn't the point. There will forever be people who judge you if you are public about your situation. There might be people who say you shouldn't minister or that you shouldn't remarry. These things can happen whether you get divorced or not, so while they should not be a deciding factor, they should make you aware that your status with some might change.

Divorce can also be a financial killer, which means if you have spent years in ministry with financial backing, your financial situation may easily change. If you have children you may have to go to work or take on an additional job, or you may have to scale your ministry back to accommodate what is financially feasible for you. This is not to say your ministry can't grow or can't handle a personal financial setback. If you have a ministry that is entirely independent of your personal finances that's great, and not something to worry about. A change in your personal finances, however, could easily impact your ability to travel, to give to other ministries or to ministry projects, and to plan a financial forecast in a long-term future.

Perhaps the most relevant thing above all others with divorce is the demand on spiritual and personal adjustments that come along with such a situation. Divorce is hard on everyone, even though it is not life-threatening (no one ever died from divorce). The difficulties can cause a pause in your desire to minister, and you may find you need to receive ministry from a good leader. If you are looking to get divorced, it's important you have support, including non-judgmental ministers who can help hold you up, encouraging you to rest when you need it and keep going when you are ready to run your race again.

Much of the way a divorce impacts your ministry relates to how you handle yourself in your ministry capacity. Ministry isn't the place to involve everyone as you behave in a messy manner. What happens in the details of your divorce is between you and your spouse, not you and everyone in your ministry. As much as possible, keep family drama out of your ministry.

While there are positives and negatives to divorce, none of these cancel one another out. Positives don't mean you should stay, and negatives don't mean you should leave. In the end, the decision to dissolve your marriage is between you and your spouse. You must rely on your judgment about your situation because you are the one who is in it. No ministry persona or image is worth the unending pain and difficulty of a bad marriage. I considered divorce in my own situation, but in the end, divorce was not the right decision for me. I have also met ministers who struggled in ministry after divorce, but when it was the right thing for them to do, they came back and flourished. There are many in ministry who do awesome work when they leave their spouses and find new vision, spiritual hope, and promise because their marital situations were toxic.

Faced with this difficult decision, I will be praying for you. I know God will lead you to do the right thing for your situation, and that you will be able to overcome any difficulties that might come with the territory. You've got this because God's got you!

I AM DIVORCED. CAN I BE IN MINISTRY?

Divorce is an issue of constant challenge for the church. It is the modern church's desire to uphold certain concepts of family, but we've forgotten that "family" doesn't just always fit a political or socioeconomic "norm." There are all kinds of families and all kinds of relationships, and that doesn't mean any family is of less quality than another. The same is true of divorce: it might not be the most ideal or desired circumstance, but such still exists. It's also very possibly a situation a minister may find themselves in when called into ministry.

There is absolutely no reason why a divorced individual should be disqualified from ministry on those grounds. If there is some reason why you are not properly governing your household (or why things right now are otherwise disorganized in your life), that is a different matter. If you have things reasonably together, there is no reason why you should experience any sort of prohibition on expanding or working in ministry. This doesn't mean you won't encounter questions or people who, at times, make an issue out of divorce that shouldn't exist, but know that if you are called to ministry, there is no reason you can't serve as a divorced individual.

You may need to find a leadership or church that does not see divorce as an issue. This may mean not remaining where you've been for a while. I would recommend prayer for your best course of action and for direction to a supportive community (if you are not already a part of one) that will train you for where you need to be and will support you in your ministry call, irrespective of your divorce.

For more on the Biblical specifics as to divorce and the Christian, check out the question I answered earlier, *I'm contemplating a divorce. How will this impact my ministry?*

I FEEL SO LONELY AS A MINISTER. WHAT ARE SOME SOLUTIONS?

Loneliness is a common experience for ministers. Alienation is one of many complicated facets of leadership. We tend to spend much of our time with those we lead, which means there is a certain boundary between us and them. Spouses don't always understand, family members can become contrary to the work, and ministers aren't the friendliest or trusting group of people. Ministers can be a judgmental bunch, thus causing those who don't fit in very well with the established cliques to retreat, finding themselves lonely.

Being a leader, especially if you are one in the context of being a leader's leader (apostle or prophet) is not an easy task. Accomplishing the needed guidance, advice, and interaction to lead others requires a certain level of separation, both from the immediate individual and from people in general. Being a leader is more than just preaching the Gospel in pulpits. If you are working with people, they need counseling, personal advice and interaction, education, and structure, all implemented with the hope and inspiration needed to launch them into the place where they are supposed to be. We can't do this if we are littered down with many voices and burdens. Thus, distance and time is a must for any minister.

This doesn't change the fact that ministry can be a very lonely place. The best way to combat this is to seek God for quality, rather than quantity, in your friendships, relationships, and spiritual development. Having a great leader can take some of the strain and burden out of ministry loneliness, especially when you have questions or needs to sort out. It's also essential to pray for God to lead you to people who can be your friends, understanding what you are dealing with, speaking into your life, and lifting you up when you need it. In the reverse, you need to be able to offer the same to your friends so that friendships remain mutual and edifying.

As ministers, it's also important to pursue outside interests and hobbies. Sometimes it feels like the only place we go to is church, the only thing we do is church, and the only people we see are church. Taking a class, going to a movie, taking a break, going out to eat, seeing a show, and doing new and different things are all important aspects of life and living. We should never forget how important it is to live beyond the confines of ministry as we go about our lives.

I would also encourage you to take your loneliness to God and see if there are some relationship changes you need to make in your life. I know that I spent many years lonely in ministry because I pursued wrong relationships, thinking they would amount to something or somehow better me in the long run. They didn't. It just always felt like an uphill battle; I was always making overtures and efforts without any reciprocation. If you are always pursuing your friends or those around you, maybe it's time to consider that you have outgrown those people. Allow God to lead you to a new place, a new start, and a new community for this time and season in your life.

There Are People Who Have Left My Ministry Who Now Want to Come Back. How Do I Handle This Situation?

When people leave our ministries, we usually have feelings about it. Whether the feelings range from anger over the circumstances to concerns about finances (and everything in between), ministry departures are usually seldom met with joy and dancing. Even under the best of circumstances, feelings are usually a little hard. Departures remind a leader they are not perfect, no matter how hard they might work to establish a great church or ministry there will always be those who find the ministry unsuitable, and it can easily feel like personal failure.

As one minister to another, having people leave, decide the ministry isn't for them, or even those who feel wronged and storm out in anger or judgment are all inevitable. They are part of being a leader, growing pains of ministry experience, and the reality is that not everyone likes everyone or everything, even in ministry. It's unrealistic to think everyone will like us or want to be part of what we do for God. Even though we are in ministry and supposedly working with other Christians, it's completely unrealistic to assume everyone will conduct departures and disagreements with proper conduct. Being a leader means having to make unpopular decisions, take stands, deal with things people don't want to deal with, and all of that can combine, no matter how Christian, empathetic, or great you've been with everyone, to serious issues that can cause dissention and upset in your ministry.

How you handle someone who wants to return to a

ministry, therefore, relates to how they left. If someone left on good terms or due to a move or personal issue (nothing that has to do with the ministry at hand), having them return is not a big deal. Having someone who left under discorded or dismissal conditions, especially if the one who left felt things were unfair or unjust, adds a whole new dimension to a ministry return. When people typically return to a ministry, they assume they'll have their prior position or a promotion, they expect to be welcomed back with a smile and nary a consequence for leaving...but is this realistic?

When people desire to return to our ministry and they've left in the face of dismissal, of having their papers stripped, or they left in a childish tantrum, I take into careful consideration the reasons for the return. If I am in position to have to do stern things in the face of a ministry disagreement, someone has done something bad enough to rate such. Not everyone who has ever left our ministry did so on bad terms. There were some instances that no matter how much I might have tried to make sure others left on good terms, it didn't happen because it wasn't all up to me. If someone is coming back, we'd like to assume they have seen the error of their ways and are ready to move forward into new territory. Such is not always the case. We leaders need to keep two things in mind with returns. The first is those who are under our care at present, and our own good judgment in the face of such situations. We can't let someone return to our work with full-standing and wreak havoc on those who are there now. We cannot allow our ministries to suffer the poison of embitterment or hostility, and we cannot, as leaders, keep going through the same things with people over and over again. So how do we handle these situations?

There are three components necessary for such a return: discussion, repentance and amends, and repayment. If these three components are met, then reinstatement is in order.

- **Discussion** requires the individual or individuals to come to you directly, as their leader. They must acknowledge they have caused harm to others, whether you or someone else in the ministry, either directly or indirectly on account of their bad behavior. This may have happened while part of the ministry, in their departure, or after they left. This is not a mediocre "I'm sorry" conversation. By coming directly, they establish an open line of communication for forgiveness and reconciliation. By doing so, they acknowledge they have done wrong, and they desire to do whatever is required to make things right.

- **Repentance and amends** dictate they are aware they were in the wrong, they desire to change whatever it was that they did, and they seek to make any wrong situations right again (inasmuch as they are able to do so). If they made statements against you or your ministry to others, they notify others they lied, exaggerated, or told untruths. In keeping with this, they make public statements to that effect. They also state they will no longer seek to defame or discredit any leadership or individual within the ministry and publicly apologize for doing so. In this particular instance, it's not wise to just take someone's word they will do it. You need to see evidence of it in action, noting statements and behaviors toward repentance.

- **Repayment** involves righting the different wrongs that went beyond gossip or slander. It's understood that in their return, they will not just be granted their old position or automatic status in the ministry, but will start from the beginning, express dedication, and work their way up again. If money is owed or was promised, it will be paid; if things were stolen, they will either be returned or the cost thereof will be repaid to the ministry or to the individuals involved.

If someone is serious about returning and making things right, they will be willing to discuss, repent and amend, and repay. If they take these steps, that means they should rightly be reinstated as part of the ministry. Maybe not in the same capacity as before, but in some respect. If they are unwilling, that answers any questions about the veracity of their desire to return.

HOW DO I HANDLE CONFLICTS IN MY CHURCH?

Conflicts are an inevitable part of church life. Whenever you work with a group of people, someone isn't going to like someone else, someone isn't going to get along with someone else, and someone is going to carry themselves in such a manner that makes others not like them. It's just part of human nature: whenever you get people together, they don't all get along. We love the idea of reciting Bible verses and hope that doing so will cause people to dial back their negativity, but unfortunately, this doesn't always work. Conflict has human issues at its root, which means when confronted with it, leaders must roll up their sleeves and lead, all the while making sure people examine their own role and personality issues as we keep the focus on our goal at hand.

Conflicts are always different and always the same. The subject matter of conflicts varies depending on situations, and that subject matter may or may not be relevant to the conflict. The issue behind the conflict, however, is always the same. It is people's inability to stand through situations when they don't like one another or just don't see things the same way. We can't hope this will go away by itself, but must make sure that when these situations arise, we address a combination of the subject matter and the issue by doing the following:

- **Be fair** – In most situations, our discernment leads us to the right and wrong behind the argument. It's great to rely on this, but when dealing with people we can't simply write a brush stroke across their thoughts and feelings. We must be fair, hearing both sides of the situation and gain insight from what is spoken to assist and enhance our practical discernment. Listening, not playing favorites, and establishing that you are there for both (or all) parties is most essential to seeing a conflict resolved.

- **Administer a sense of justice rather than just trying to make the situation go away** – Justice means doing what is right rather than what might be easy. This might mean forcing the individuals involved to work out their issues themselves, to keep them working on the same project but expecting a change of attitude and causing both to look inside themselves and the pride that keeps them from working with and helping others productively. The two people might never like each other, be friends outside of the project, or come to be true buddies, but a sense of justice requires both to be insightful about doing right in the future.

- **Be trustworthy** – It's tempting to throw people out of your office when they act bad (and yes, sometimes this is warranted), telling them to grow up and stop acting like they are, but this has a way of being very counter-productive in the long run. If those who come to you feel that they can't confide in you or bring their issues to you, that will equate to a lack of trust in the long term. Keep matters confidential, just as if this was a situation involving counseling, and encourage long-term growth from it.

- **Encourage others to work out their issues with one another** – Unless you are a children's or youth minister, those you lead are not children. Our ultimate goal with those we lead should be to help them see issues within themselves and resolve conflicts among themselves, honestly and openly. Everyone should be encouraged to apologize when wrong, make amends as necessary, and graciously accept apologies and amends when they arise.

Conflicts should never, ever overtake a ministry or a minister to the point where practical, ministerial work cannot be done properly. If you are experiencing an intense bout of conflicts between people in your ministry, it's best to handle things one at a time, encourage people to work out their differences, and expect that they will do so. Maintain a voice of fairness, but at the same time, be a little stern in your expectation that everyone will conduct themselves properly. If conflicts get so out of hand that things don't work properly, then it is expected one (or both) will step back from the assignment at hand and will allow the work to go forward.

Instead of avoiding the topic, I encourage ministers to discuss matters relating to conflict from the pulpit and in Bible studies, with the sincere expectation that before conflict ever arises, congregants will be on alert for their own behavior and attitudes that are less-than-stellar. If we recognize our own tendencies toward pride, combativeness, selfishness, and insistence on having things our own way, we will be far better aware of ways that conflicts can arise from our own negative behavior. If we all examine ourselves, we will all be better for it when it comes to working well and sorting issues with others.

Should We Allow LGBTQ+ People Into Our Ministries?

Many years ago, I had a friend on Yahoo Messenger who lived in the far away state of West Virginia (I was in New York at the time). We didn't talk for very long, but long enough to have an interesting conversation about LGBTQ+ inclusion in church. At the time, the issue of gay inclusion was new in our churches, just starting to come into mainstream view. The major opposition wasn't just against gay marriage, but in many ways seeking to eliminate gay individuals from church all together. There was a lot of rhetoric about how to keep kids from becoming gay and about how to identify gay people, sending otherwise normal people on unspeakable witch hunts. Accusations were sometimes made that might or might not have been true. I remember my friend asking one day, "How do you feel about gay people in church?" I hadn't been asked this so pointe blank before. We started to discuss the issue, and something he said to me stuck with me: "The church is God's house. How can we tell someone they can't come in God's house?"

This stuck with me through many years and many challenges to the views I might have had on the subject. As much as we like to shout that "all are welcome" and that people should "come as you are," much of the church doesn't really mean it. Churches call other church members, hoping they will leave their existing church to attend that church. When someone who doesn't quite fit into the picture shows up, no one knows what to do about that. Whether deliberate or not, those who aren't a perfect match for a church's ideals and concepts aren't made to feel very comfortable being there, and eventually, they either stop coming or just don't make the commitment to come at all.

Let's start by defining a few things that will make my answer to this question a little clearer. "LGBTQ+" is an abbreviation for Lesbian, Gay, Bisexual, Transgender, and Queer. The plus sign indicates all others who are part of the queer community, referring to anyone who does not fall into the standard combination of heterosexual and cisgender (identifying as their biological gender identified at birth). It's important to realize the queer community is far more than just "gay people" or "transgender people," as some communities lead us to believe. Under the "rainbow banner" are several different ideas about gender, identity, and sexuality. The queer community includes everyone from individuals who identify as polysexual to asexual, and everything from romantic relationships to aromantic ones. There isn't one exclusive identity. Even within the queer community, there is sometimes question about who belongs and how things are defined, as terminology continues to evolve.

It's very possible for individuals to be part of the queer community and not realize it because they think in terms of the binaries of gay and straight. It's also not uncommon for people to falter in language when it comes to identity and not know they are queer because they don't have the right terminology to identify themselves.

In saying all this, there's another very important detail: queer individuals have existed throughout time. There have been queer people in God's Kingdom since God has had a Kingdom. There might not have been language to describe the way such individuals identified and processed their own attractions, but such has always been a thing. To try and eliminate such individuals from church – no matter what the logic might be therein – is impossible.

I think asking who we should or shouldn't allow in our ministries is an example where it's not the answer that's the issue, but the question itself. There is nothing in Scripture that dictates we get to engineer church according to our own likes, dislikes, and comforts. Jesus Himself called to everyone because everyone is a sinner. Whether or not we acknowledge it, we all have some form of sin in our lives. This means to exclude anyone – no matter what you may think of them – is excluding someone from hearing the Gospel message. In doing so, you are deciding who is or is not worthy to know God for themselves.

In the book of Acts, the eunuch who has just heard of Christ asks: What doth hinder me to be baptized? In other words, he was asking the Evangelist Philip, "What's stopping me from taking the next step in my faith?" The answer back was nothing. There was water, there was a willing evangelist, and there was a willing faith within the eunuch (who would fall on the "queer" spectrum). Whether it was of his own doing, it related to something in his own sexual identity, or it had been done to him against his will, the eunuch did not fall into the societal "norm" of heterosexual attraction and gender identity. Nobody stood there and asked him if he was gay, if he needed to take a church class to be baptized, or if he was going to become straight and "normal" when he came up out of the water. They simply said, you know what, there is nothing to hinder this move of faith – and they baptized him. So, my question to you is: what doth hinder? I know I don't want the answer to be me – and I am sure you don't want the answer to be that you were a hinderance.

It's my personal opinion that it doesn't matter what you think of individuals in the queer community. Communities do not have to be the same, one-note figures to thrive. It's not your job to form an opinion about anyone else. It's the same no matter what the subject matter might be, whether it's an unwed mother or a single parent or a searching teenager or the seemingly happy couple who has everything wrong in their personal lives. It's not our job to hinder someone from hearing about the Gospel and receive what God has for them. We never know what God wants to do in someone else's life, or how He might want to do it through us, so we must be open to the possibility, to the idea that whoever comes and receives from what we have to offer is welcome there.

Instead of asking who you should let in, start asking how you can better let everyone know they are welcome in your ministry, and how you can show this truly welcoming spirit to anyone who is interested in coming to receive whatever it is that God has for them in this special place.

How do we counsel LGBTQ+ individuals?

Counseling an individual who is part of the "queer spectrum" requires a professional approach, one that echoes a certain level of understanding and non-judgment. It is not the position of a minister to form a personal opinion about what one does and try to impose personal views on the client. Your job is to be there for that person, to listen to their concerns, to hear them speak, and to offer methods and suggestions to help them discover for themselves whatever they seek.

In other words: we counsel LGBTQ+ individuals the same way we counsel anyone else. While some of the peripheral issues may be a little different, the method and approach is the same. We poise ourselves as good listeners and we help the person we counsel to discover things about themselves that will lead to empowered decision-making.

It's not a big secret that LGBTQ+ church inclusion is a controversial issue. If you are someone who has a heart – and a call – for those who identify as such, you are already ahead of the game. Through your work, you can establish a pattern of trust and acceptance. Throughout the years, LGBTQ+ individuals have suffered through church therapies that were unprofessional and dangerous. Such practices were (and are) cruel, inhumane, and ineffective. Aversion therapy, shock therapy, reorientation therapy, and mutilation are abusive and morally wrong. While there are still programs that promise to "cure" someone's orientation, they are all unproven and unscientific, and in the long run, cause more harm, shame, and pain to individuals looking for help.

What I would tell you to do is counsel an LGBTQ+

individual the exact same way that you would anyone else who comes to you. Instead of using counseling as a ploy to try and change them, use counseling as an opportunity to help them find a better sense of themselves and equip them with techniques and abilities to help them solve problems and issues that may arise throughout their lives. As you create a safe, trustworthy place, you will find you will help people – maybe not in the way you imagined – but in a way that is edifying and encouraging to them. That is our ultimate call through counseling, helping people to develop a better sense of themselves, and to do so without judgment or criticism in our practice.

How do we respond to transgender and non-binary individuals who desire to use pronouns different from their gender of origin?

Being transgender and what is classified as "non-binary" seems to be a new issue in our times but in reality, it is not. In fact, history is full of people who have identified as a different gender from the biological sex they might have been born with, or do not identify with their gender identified at birth. Given there are hundreds of intersex conditions that are not always obvious or visible, it is not just likely, but reality, that such individuals have existed throughout time. Gender development is not a simple process, and in many instances, human beings are not as simple as being male or female. There are a wide range of developments, understandings, and complexities to the process, and they can render differences that cause someone to identify differently than what might seem obvious, or not obvious in an individual.

But, before we examine the question, let's discuss the issues at hand, and understand gender a little bit better.

Biological sex, gender and gender identity are three different things. Biological sex is the sexual assignment one has at birth, although there can be many variations in how this is designated. Because we cannot always see gender variations in someone by looking at them, it is very possible that what may appear to be "biological" may not, in fact, be how it appears. In its simplest assignment, biological sex is something one is "declared" at birth and usually falls into one of two binary categories: male or female.

Gender, in its strictest definition, relates to the different characteristics that define things, such as being male or female. Gender can be both biological and conditional. The way we often understand gender is not neutral, as society assigns certain likes, dislikes, and characteristics to us based on gender conditioning. For example, the stereotypes that girls aren't supposed to like sports and boys aren't supposed to like cooking would fall into the category of societal conditioning as pertains to gender. It's not that either thing has anything to do with one's biological gender, but society often tells us – and assigns such things – to gender. This means that gender, in and of itself, can be a confusing thing as it is associated with far more than biology.

Gender identity, as the third marker, is how one identifies with their assigned gender. They may identify as male or female or not fall into either spectrum. Those who do not accept the binary definition are classified as "non-binary."

I am explaining this as simply as possible, while acknowledging my explanations may be too simplistic for some and not simplistic enough for others. The reality is that biological sex, gender, and gender identity don't always align in a nice, neat package. Most people in this world do find their sex, gender, and gender identity to align, at least for the most part. There may be things about their gender, spoken of in stereotypes that they do not accept, but for the most part, they do not find any conflict between their body, their assigned gender, and their minds.

However, this is not the case for everyone. If a person has been raised or conditioned as one gender but feel they should be a different one (as in a male believing he should be female, non-binary, or agender, or vice versa), that individual would be classified as transgender. Being transgender is described by people in different ways. Some express it as feeling as if they are born in the wrong body or trapped in the wrong body. Some describe it as having the mind of the opposite sex, but the body of their biological sex. No one is quite certain what causes someone to be transgender, but because of the vast possibilities in intersex conditions, it is very likely it has its origins in biology. There is no way someone can condition another person to be transgender; it is just something that exists, and no one really understands how or why.

Individuals who don't readily accept the identity and norms of either gender fall into the "non-binary" spectrum, which is part of the transgender spectrum. They may identify with the opposite gender, or with parts of one gender and parts of another, or with neither at all. Some people fall in the "gender fluid" category, which means they blend what they consider to be the best or most identifiable of binary or all genders into themselves.

Those who identify differently than their biological sex or gender at birth may decide to have a process of transition; some do not. Some are content to identify differently or in a non-binary fashion. Not everyone desires to be identified differently than what gender may seem obvious to others, but some do. Some may change their names to match their identity or modify the ones they have, and some desire to be referred to by different pronouns than that of their assigned birth origin.

I believe it is most prudent to ask people what they want to be called and what pronouns they prefer to use, especially when meeting someone new. We often get very tripped up over technicalities, but there is nothing wrong with acknowledging how someone sees themselves and what they desire to be called. Honoring someone's name shows respect and honor to that person, their process and experience. We are here to be catalysts for their spiritual process, wherever that may take them. It's not for us to decide or judge how they identify, but to love them, because they are human beings who need the Gospel as much as anyone else does.

Instead of being concerned about things such as biology, assignments, and labels, we need to be interested in souls, which do not have specified gender assignments to them. When we do this, we can see more of where God has for us to be, more of how diversity fits into the spiritual spectrum God calls us to embrace, and how we can better love people, right where they are, as they are.

WHAT IS POLYANDRY AND HOW DO I HANDLE POLYANDROUS COUNSELING?

Polyandry means "many attractions." It is a relationship dynamic involving at least three people (or more) in a committed relationship. The exact practice of polyandry varies, and you may encounter a variety of different situations under the polyandry heading. In some situations, all parties are intimately involved with one another; in others, one person is involved with multiple partners; and in others, where all people in the relationship are involved with others, but the others are not involved with those in the relationship dynamic.

We could define polyandry as a modern approach to the polygamous relationships we see in Scripture, such as with Jacob, Leah, and Rachel, Solomon and his many wives (although I've never heard of a polyandrous relationship involving so many people), or David and his multiple wives. There are some differences, the main one being polyandry doesn't require the exclusivity of a woman while a man has multiple women. In polyandry, any partner of any gender is free to take multiple partners, also of any gender (depending on the terms set by the individual) and explore different relationships. Polyamorous arrangements may involve divided time during the week, joint living arrangements, or separate living situations. Polyamorous individuals may also be single, committed, married, have a primary partner or more than one partner on a regular basis, or may be long-distance or live in the same area. As many polyamorous situations exist, there are different relationship terms and rules, which most adapt in their unique situations.

It's not a secret that polyandry can create complicated issues for relationship boundaries, intimacy, and unique circumstances we might see in monogamous relationships, only amped up due to the situation. If someone is coming for counseling, there are, most likely, different issues they seek to address, be they within themselves or their group dynamic. These might involve communication, intimacy, jealousy, and commitment. There are many reasons why such relationships can be complicated, but those are often the reasons someone might seek out polyandry. They may very well desire the challenge of sorting out issues like jealousy, maintaining communication, commitment, and a greater sense of intimacy.

What we should note is that much like counseling a queer individual isn't that different from counseling anyone else, counseling a polyandrous individual or group isn't that different from counseling a monogamous one. Many of the issues are the same as any other relationship situation, they are just managed a little differently.

We need to remember the purpose in counseling to help people discover what is best for themselves and how to make better decisions in their relationships. This means you offer insights and techniques for someone to do just that. Judgment and criticism probably won't get you very far. No matter how you feel about the issue, avoid the temptation to use it to push your own ideas. Be professional; serve in the capacity desired. If you are sought out, it is due to trust. If you handle counseling in the same way you would any other situation, there will be no doubt your time will positively impact those who come and seek out your skill.

How do I handle ministry-related conflicts in my home?

By "ministry conflicts in my home," I assume you are referring to specific issues that arise within your household as result of your ministry. Much like conflicts that might arise at church or work, they are marked by tensions or disagreements. These conflicts typically have one person in common, and that is you. This can make you feel awkward or out of place, like you are in position to constantly defend yourself. Not surprising, such can become exhausting and can make you rethink both your ministry and household situation.

Constant conflict equates with a lack of support from those around you. The occasional conflict is normal and is to be expected from time to time. Humans are humans and ministry is ministry, and the combination of the two means postponed nights out, help with the kids, missing dinner, or not making it home at a regular hour. This can become grating, especially if it happens often in a given period. Being able to accept the feelings we have when our work interferes with our home lives is important. If we are going to be in ministry and married, we must learn to negotiate, set boundaries, and consider the feelings of others when "stuff happens."

On the other hand, when we are in ministry and married, our partners need to respect and understand things are going to come up that require our response or presence, and that means plans will be interrupted. Sometimes it seems like all we experience is interruption to our personal plans. As with all things related to ministry, we must be present when such is required. Our spouses should see that occasional sacrifice of time or helping with household tasks as a contribution to the Lord's service.

Before you do anything rash (like deciding you don't want to be in ministry or marriage anymore) approach the impending household conflicts much like you would any other conflict: listen to the complaints, assess the needs versus the realities of the situation, find reasonable solutions, and act accordingly. Many ministerial household conflicts are a result of miscommunication or misunderstanding, and it's important to correct misconceptions, stand up for the principles of ministry, and examine areas of needed balance required for your own well-being and the well-being of your family.

Those who live with ministers must understand that we aren't always available in the same way a spouse not in ministry might be. At the same time, we must never pursue ministry to the neglect of everyone and everything else in our lives. If you have found that balance in a reasonable semblance of understanding, that's great. Don't worry too much about the occasional times when life happens. If you haven't found it, now is a great time to start. Either way, emphasize that no matter what is going on, you need the support of your family to keep everything functional.

What Political Positions Should I Hold as a Christian Minister?

It's been about sixty years since the predominately white Evangelical Christian world entered the realm of conservative United States politics. Those who are a part of churches throughout the country have experienced a wild ride as a result. The waves of propaganda stemming from their helm: Christians need to be politically active; conservative (often associated with Republicans) American politics are associated with Christian values' the United States is a "Christian nation" and that identity is the same as white Evangelical Christianity; and that failure to see things from said viewpoint renders one a questionable Christian (or not one at all). Such has caused many believers to question their faith. There are many who go to church and feel out of place, some don't know what to make of these trends, and there are those who are staunchly opposed to them. In the long run, there is only one way we can define what politics have done to the church: it causes confusion.

I believe the standard conservative politics are often a great challenge for many ministers. This is especially true for female and queer ministers. American conservatism discourages women from working or holding positions of authority, believing they are best suited in the home as mothers and wives, and not good for much else. Many take issue with queer individuals, fighting against gay rights, transgender equality, and gay marriage. Many advocate to defund clinics, women's centers, and health initiatives under the guise of being against abortion and transgender care. They push against curriculums and defunding school

190

programs. This is not to say there aren't flaws in more liberal politics, but because Christianity has espoused conservatism as its identifying point, we aren't going to talk about liberal politics. Looking over the landscape of conservatism, it is not Biblical nor Christian, but the creation of an American system based on American values, trying very hard to win Christian voters by pretending such is "Christian."

I have yet to meet anyone who is all conservative or liberal, even in church. Most do lean more one way than the other, but when it comes to certain ideals and concepts, everyone's perspectives are unique. The ministers I've met who try to fit in the conservative box always pay a very heavy price to do so. It is because it means keeping up unforgiving appearances to make sure others believe they are as perfect and ideal as the values they claim to espouse. This is harmful to ministers, not to mention those they minister to, as they try to make this perfect image their goal. In the process, many problems, issues, hurt and needed healing go undone and unrecognized, in the favor of keeping up with the Joneses.

As a minister, I would encourage you to stand Scriptural, rather than across party lines. If that means you don't adopt political positions, that's what it will have to mean. We should never preach politics; only the heart of Christ and things Christ desires us to know. As I write this, the United States is in a heated battle between liberals and conservatives, democrats and republicans. The whole thing shows no sign of stopping. As resistance grows against the main administration, people resort to equally disturbing behaviors and attitudes to try and prove their point. The endless back and forth is exhausting, not to mention quickly gets out of control. Everyone is in it to win it, and the more issues escalate, the more likely they are to grow out of control.

As a Christian minister, I advise to keep politics out of

ministry for a few reasons. First, politics vary across different social demographics, ethnic groups, social classes, and genders, because all feel different issues should be governmental priorities. Someone who is unemployed is more interested in job creation and unemployment benefits than a wealthy benefactor who inherited a company they don't even have to start or take care of themselves. What do both people have in common? They both need the Gospel, so one is more giving with what they have to the one who does not have, and the one who does not have can receive encouragement and hope to continue moving forward. Our message is not a political wrangling so the government will solve all our problems, but that those who have should share with those who don't have, and that somewhere, some way, we can continue in this work of the Gospel to bring all to salvation.

Politics also vary from country to country, so it's wrong to think you can safely espouse certain political viewpoints if you are ministering to an international audience. Not everyone feels the same way about social issues on an international platform, and what may seem obvious to someone in one country may not be in another because they have different laws, rules, governances, and priorities. If you want to reach people beyond borders, you need to preach beyond borders, which requires a global understanding of the human condition, human need, and an empathy for the different things people face worldwide.

As a Christian minister, you certainly believe in social responsibilities, duties to the downtrodden, community involvement, and an empowerment of the lives of those you serve. This may influence your politics, and it is your prerogative to back candidates as an individual who share these important principles. As a Christian minister, however, you should never endorse candidates or tell those you lead to be politically involved or affiliated with a certain party or candidate. We are still a part of a greater Kingdom. As a Christian minister, you can work to make that a reality, because such won't happen through a secular nation – but through the spiritual Kingdom set up and established by Jesus Christ, Himself. In the meantime, we make it real and alive every single day: through our values, through the work we do to benefit others, and ultimately, through living and proclaiming the Gospel.

I WANT TO BE A GOOD ROLE MODEL IN ALL AREAS OF MY LIFE. HOW DOES MINISTRY IMPACT MY SEX LIFE?

I'm a big advocate of ministerial privacy. It seems like the second we assume a leadership role everyone thinks they are entitled to a piece of our lives. Over time, those pieces quickly add up and can leave us feeling void of any sense self. Answering invasive questions, offering too much information, and doing all of this in the name of some sort of "transparency proof" (that we have nothing to hide) is causing leaders to lose credibility, dignity, and privacy in their own lives.

If you are married and your spouse is aware you are in ministry, it shouldn't change your intimate life that much, if at all. You are still a part of a married couple and being in ministry might change some of the peripherals, but it doesn't introduce a lot of change to your intimate life. Unless there is something decidedly ungodly in your intimate life (such as spousal rape), there shouldn't be any reason why your sexual experience changes. If there are peripheral issues (such as tension over chores or lack of presence in the house) those may cause issues, but there is no reason why your sex life should change because of your ministry.

In any situation, what you do or don't do in your sex life classifies under the heading of ministerial privacy. This is not a license to have orgies, affairs, or a bunch of one-night stands. We still believe in being good role models and upholding a certain level of dignity and respect for ourselves when it comes to sex, but this doesn't mean what you do in your private life in any sense is anyone's business but your own.

The Bible doesn't supply us with a long list of dos and don'ts when it comes to sexual expressions between couples, and that means we don't need to account for such personal matters with others. It also means when such matters arise, we don't need to volunteer or offer specific information about ourselves.

A few words of note: it's not wise to take up with members of your congregation or to "date through" your church. I've known ministers who have done this and it's not a good idea. It erodes your leadership foundations as well as creating massive conflict among members. Leaving your sex life out of your ministry means upholding a professional boundary and not crossing such intimate lines with those you lead.

This doesn't mean we can't talk about sexuality or sexual matters as ministers; it just means we take our own personal selves out of the discussion. It also means we don't put anyone on the spot about sexuality or sexual matters, be that in the pulpit, sermons, or other situations. If people are having issues or someone needs to discuss such an issue, counseling and the elders of the church exist for a reason. Offering too much personal detail doesn't make you a bad person, but one that doesn't respect the boundaries of others as well as your own. Recognizing this isn't something you need to announce to your ministry should take pressure off and enable you to explore your intimate life as is wise and best for you.

AS PUBLIC FIGURES, HOW MUCH SHOULD WE GO THROUGH TO MAINTAIN A YOUTHFUL APPEARANCE?

I am not upset that you've asked this question, but that we must ask it. It bothers me that we resist the concept of aging and feel we must compete with young people, even in church. It's hard enough to struggle with aging in general culture, but the idea we now have to stay young forever in church adds a new dimension to the issue.

It's not a secret that aging isn't well-accepted in society. Pressures abound to have cosmetic surgery, alter one's appearance, dye gray hair, remain a certain weight, and dress in youthful fashions. Anything associated with aging – be it lines or wrinkles on skin, gray hair, weight gain, and changes in the body – are considered unattractive and distasteful. The expectation, therefore, is to try and look younger.

It disturbs me that these different trends of worldly vanity are now a part of the church. While we claim to value wisdom and experience, we want that wisdom and experience to come in a package that's not designed to house those things. We love the concept of generations of parents and grandparents and being able to stand proud before an assembly, but we don't like the idea of looking like parents and grandparents. The immensity of contradictions is scary, yet too familiar in the church we serve.

I once heard it said that your appearance should be the least interesting thing about you. I believe we need to be comfortable with ourselves as we are, learning to embrace the body shape and appearance we have. Our appearance should reflect who we are, as an expression of that. How you choose to do this is your choice, and there's no shame in being real about your age, your weight, your physique, and who you are, right now. If you want to take care of your skin, color your hair, wear make-up, or do something else to accentuate more of who you are, go for it. If there's something you want to do, then do it. But don't feel like you must conform to an abstract concept of youth, subjecting yourself to plastic surgery, clothes that are uncomfortable, or to competing younger people. You are your age, and you are beautiful at your age, no matter what it is. Embrace it as a part of you and it will make your message to those you minister to that much better and more believable.

I WANT TO REACH OUT TO MY COMMUNITY. HOW DO I DO THIS?

I laud you for desiring to impact your community, right where you are. Many in ministry have lofty concepts about influencing others without considering how such influence begins. I'm sure the members of your community will be blessed by your outreach, and that it'll change the face of your community for good.

One of the major reasons Christian ministries fail to engage their communities is due to monotone perspectives. Ministers take a couple of Bible texts that appear to be on a topic, develop an event around that topic (even though it's probably been done before), hand out the same advice that's been handed out before. Ministries go on in this same pattern with no consideration or aforethought as to what to do or how it's being done. Ministry is not a matter of promoting distant or irrelevant advice but speaking to the issues that people have in their lives right now and being of service to them, making sure their souls are touched as we care about others.

The first thing every individual who desires to do outreach should do is their homework. I know homework isn't a lot of fun, but it is often the space between a successful project and an unsuccessful one. What are the major demographics of people in your area? Are they married, single, older, or younger? What are the major issues that concern them? Different areas have different groups of people, with different needs. We should never assume to know just who is out there without doing some practical research into the situations that surround us.

Once you've done that, be creative in planning an event

that will positively bless the people in your area with information, education, and spiritual edification. Don't shy away from controversial subjects! Bring in experts, examine issues seldom explored at church. In preaching, pick Bible topics that will edify and inform rather than providing a message that can be heard anywhere else at any time. Offer an experience that isn't like any other, and you will find that those in your area will respond to it.

No matter what you decide to do, open your ideas about ministry so you can recognize the needs that exist. Stand as a place of service for them. If you do that, no matter what specific issue or issues you seek to take on, your ministry – and community – will be better for it.

Is it all right to not want to be in ministry?

Yes, it certainly is. The Scriptures teach us we all have different gifts and abilities. If God has not called you to be in ministry, it's perfectly normal not to desire to assume such a position. If you know you are called and are avoiding your calling that is a different matter altogether, but I am not going on that premise. Knowing the world we live in, the situations we face, and the pressures to achieve, I'm understanding public ministry is something you don't feel called to do. If this is the case, it is perfectly fine, normal, and honorable for you to refrain from pursuing a public ministry.

While it's true that public ministry isn't for everyone, ministry, or service – is indeed for everyone, even those who are not in public ministry. I do agree there is a huge push for people to be in ministry (even if they aren't called to do so) and such pressure can be very intense. Even if you are not called to pursue preaching or church ministry, there is still some way, something that you are called to do in your life that benefits and serves other people. It is most important you discover what that is because it is where your life's purpose will be found. You will find new ways to dive into life, even if it's not in the form of "ministry" most familiar.

In God's Kingdom there are no "greater" or "lesser" calls. If your call is to take care of your family or remain single, to work a job, to engage in some volunteer work, to help at church wherever you can, write, sing, talk to someone else, and beyond, you have the ability to make someone else's life better. If you do this however you are called, you are engaging in your own acceptable ministry service. However that manifests and however it works for you, I encourage you to go for it – because you can only serve well when you are placed in purpose and love wherever God best has for you to be.

SECTION 3:

SORTING OUT OURSELVES

Since, then, you have been raised with Christ,
set your hearts on things above, where Christ is,
seated at the right hand of God.
Set your minds on things above, not on
earthly things. For you died, and your life
is now hidden with Christ in God.
When Christ, Who is your life, appears,
then you also will appear with Him in glory.

(Colossians 3:1-4)

I BELIEVE IN COURTING RATHER THAN DATING BECAUSE IT'S MORE BIBLICAL, BUT THE MEN I MEET TELL ME I'M "TOO INTENSE." WHY IS THE CONCEPT OF COURTING SCARING OFF POTENTIAL MATES?

I am going to divide my answer into two parts. First, I am going to address the facts, and then I am going to give you my opinion as to why you may keep striking out in the relationship area. Hopefully these perspectives will give you some insight into what is going on and what others are picking up when you are involved with them.

The first thing: courting is not more Biblical than dating. Neither modern-day courting nor dating are found in the Bible. The Biblical system of betrothal and marriage is based in ancient cultural attitudes about marriage and relationships. As a rule, these attitudes are not held by people in modern times. In Bible times, marriage was a societal system based on alliances and reconciliations between families, tribes, or clans. The goal of marriage was the continuation of a race, tribe, or group. Ancient marriage's purpose was not love or romance; it was survival. For this reason, marriages were arranged by immediate families or close relatives, not by couples themselves. The ancients believed the closeness and intimacy of marriage was dependent on living day in and day out together as a couple learned how to compromise, make decisions, and engage in a sexual relationship. There was no accounting for how well couples knew each other prior to marriage; in fact, much of the time, couples didn't know each other very well, at all. Their concept of love was based on duty. The need for a couple to survive, both racially or tribally and as an immediate family, would make up for whatever might not have been there, whether that was lack of attraction, romance, interest, or love.

As a woman in Biblical times, you would have had no choice or say in who you married. Within a year of your first period, you would be forced to marry whoever your family selected for you, whether you knew him or not. It wouldn't matter if you liked him, if he was a lot older than you, if he was abusive toward you, or if he found you displeasing. No matter what happened, you had no divorce rights. He was free to do whatever he pleased and to divorce you for any reason, leaving you destitute and maybe denying the children you had together. He also had the right to take additional wives, concubines, and to frequent prostitutes if he so chose. No one had the concept of waiting for "the one" that God had for them in Biblical times because there was no such thing. You married whomever your family found most suitable. That was the beginning and end of the whole matter. That was reality of Biblical marriage.

Marriage was a difficult task as couples found ways to make life work within their ancient relationship dynamics. Yes, the Scriptures try very hard to uphold certain codes or standards, but the reality of ancient Israel is that they seldom, if ever, upheld most of these guidelines. There is no reason to romanticize marital custom in the Bible because marriages were no better, nor worse, than they are today. Marital longevity does not equate to happiness. Lack of cultural divorce options do not equate to better marriages. These peripherals create laws that make divorce harder and more improbable for people who need to escape a bad or difficult marriage.

However you engage with a potential mate in modern times it's safe to say you do not engage with them in a Biblical context. If there is anything we can learn from the Bible's marriage culture, it is that we should respect – and embrace – cultural attitudes surrounding marriage and dating. Isaac's marriage to Rebekah (his first cousin once removed) in Genesis is quite different than Mary's marriage to Joseph when she was a young teenager in Matthew's Gospel. Obviously, marital customs change. Cultural attitudes about relationships are not inherently sinful. We have the challenge of best utilizing these systems to discover what we need in a suitable mate of our choosing.

I understand why the church wants to separate its relationship values from those found among general society. The concept of courting, however, is not the solution to that problem. You probably aren't applying all the rules of "courtship" to your situation, anyhow. Unless you have a chaperone (ideally a parent or male relative) accompanying you on every outing, suggesting and approving your mates, monitoring your discussions on the phone, internet, and text, absolutely no physical contact (not kissing nor holding hands), and expecting your relationship to move along toward marriage in six months or less, you aren't practicing courtship as is understood in modern understanding. You are adopting and using the term to indicate your desire to get married instead of just dating or living with someone, and in using the term, you are using it incorrectly.

I am all for social responsibility in dating, exercising self-control, not sleeping with every person that comes along, and not using dating, living together, or a long-term relationship as excuses to not marry. I also understand when you know you are ready to get married; you might feel a certain amount of pressure toward marriage. You can, in turn, pressure those you are dating. This doesn't change the natural course of things. Before you can be ready to marry someone in our modern times, you must first know them well enough to know if that is an option for you.

Now for the opinion portion of my answer: I believe the concepts people have of modern courting is very negative and loaded with pressures that could easily scare off a potential mate. If out the gate you are making it known you want to court, that is easily going to make a potential mate run for their lives. The term comes with too much pressure to commit when they don't know who you are or if you are right for them. The expectations of courting state within one or two dates you must know whether you want to marry someone. If you still aren't sure after this time, that means they aren't right for you, and you must terminate the relationship.

Is it possible all this focus on marriage and applying pressure to make a marriage commitment takes away from the possibility of a good relationship? I say yes. I've met men who talked about marriage right away. I didn't know anything about them, and I wasn't sure if I was interested in seeing them again. Such definitely turned me off because it made me uncomfortable. In the end, I decided I didn't want to see these men again. It wouldn't matter to me how serious they were or how ready they were to get married. I didn't care if they were interested in me, because all they were interested in doing was filling a place in their lives. All the talk about me as a wife or in the role of a marriage partner, when I wasn't even sure how much I liked or felt connected to them, would make me feel as if I was being forced into something I wasn't ready to do.

We can easily see why such a situation might make me, as a woman, uncomfortable with a male. We don't seem to understand why such can make a man or other partner uncomfortable when it is perpetrated by someone else, but we should. Pressure is pressure is pressure; it doesn't matter who applies it. It's wrong for anyone to assume such a staunch upper hand in a relationship and start dictating terms and ultimatums in the form of social pressure to marry or further the relationship at a different pace. There are unspoken codes as to when it is acceptable to bring up marriage, family, and relationship issues of that nature, and this means putting such things out on the table, too early, and expecting a good result is both unfair and unreasonable.

Another potential reason for the intensity, especially in situations where courting is on the table, is the assumption that our potential partners are either exactly where we are or should be where we are. When we can't find the one we love, sometimes we try to make the one we are with who we want them to be. Sometimes it's nothing more than we are very vocal about our concepts of a mate, who they should be, what they should do, and what we expect way too early in a relationship. If a potential mate gets the early message this relationship will be about conformity, that will equate to way too much pressure.

I recognize dating is a very difficult navigational game. The whole concept of searching for "one" right person in this world for us can seem intimidating. My recommendation is to take all that out of your pursuit and focus on one person, one relationship at a time, giving things the time to see where they go and make a fair decision as to whether someone is right or wrong for you. Take a deep breath and instead of feeling pressured to marry, enjoy the journey of getting to know someone else and decide if they are suitable for you as a person. There is much to be enjoyed in dating, and instead of worrying about the end result, focus on right now: who is with you, who you are with, and take the intensity out of the relationship, deciding instead based on the individual who is in front of you, not on who wants to get married at some point down the line.

I HAVE BEEN LIVING WITH MY BOYFRIEND FOR THREE YEARS. I WANT TO GET MARRIED BUT HE DOESN'T, SO OUR RELATIONSHIP IS AT A STANDSTILL. I ALSO WANT TO DO MORE AT MY CHURCH, BUT MY PASTOR SAID FOR ME TO DO THAT, I HAVE TO GET MARRIED. WHAT DO YOU THINK OF PEOPLE LIVING TOGETHER WHO ARE NOT MARRIED?

I think to answer this question, it is better if I explain where your leader comes from and provide some things for you to think about as opposed to giving my opinion. I don't want to come between you and your pastor, nor do I want for anything I say to be seen as an excuse to undermine your pastor's governance. I also can't specifically state how I would handle your situation because I am not your leader and I don't know what instructions you have, if this is a long-standing discussion point between you and your leader, or if this is a regulation you have been informed of in the long-term. Still, I hope that what I have to offer helps you in some way to decide what is best for you in your situation.

I have been in your position in my life, and it wasn't an easy place to be. I was forced to choose in a situation that offered no good choices, and some might say the decisions I made weren't the right ones. In hindsight, I don't see my decisions as black and white, and I recognize I did the best I could at the time. Let me say straight up that getting married is not the answer to everything. In my situation, it created new problems and circumstances that I was unprepared to handle. Once I made my decision, no one from the church I attended was around to help or offer advice. I was the one left standing in situation after situation, facing difficult decisions without obvious answers. I might have tried to follow the rules but in the long run, the rules failed me. While I do not believe getting married solves all our problems, this doesn't mean marriage is bad or having rules about assuming church positions are all bad. I also believe we shouldn't treat marriage as if it's a platform for reward, something that gives us the ability to move up the ladder and serve in different ways.

Having said that, there are a couple things in your question that reveal to me a certain level of dissatisfaction in your relationship. I don't know if your pastor has taken note of those issues or not, as I don't know what you have or have not discussed with them. The way you have stated you have been living together for three years, you want to get married, but he does not, and your relationship is at a standstill are all clues to me that the relationship is in some ways displeasing to you. This doesn't mean your boyfriend is bad and you are good, or you are good, and your boyfriend is bad. It just means your relationship has hit what I call a ceiling. For a long time, you were moving toward something. One day, your movement stopped. Now your relationship can go no further than where it is unless something changes. You're in a holding pattern; your boyfriend knows you want to get married, but he doesn't, and he knows that even though you want more from your relationship, you will remain living with him. He knows you will remain even if it is hurting you, even if it is hurting your spiritual relationship, and even if it means you can't move forward in church.

To me, these issues are of far more relevance than your pastor's issue with your marital state. You have issues with your relationship itself. The issues the two of you have are deeper than whether you have a piece of paper to seal your legal union. You are also at a place where you need to decide about these issues. It doesn't sound like after three years you are able to wait and see if things get better. They are unlikely to change because your relationship has hit its ceiling.

As for your issue with your leader: if you know this is where you are called to be, then this is a rule you will have to accept. When we submit ourselves to church leadership, we give our leaders rule over us in terms of church governance and authority. They cannot force us to do anything in our private lives, but they have every right to decide how to handle what we do outside of church within its walls. This might not sound fair, but it is our leader's job to ensure the function, governance, and continuation of God's household. Their sphere of authority resides wherever it is established. Your pastor cannot force you to move out or get married, but they can say if you continue in your current state, you cannot serve in certain capacities within your congregation.

The issue of people living together without benefit of marriage is a thorny issue for most church leaders. As more people live together without the benefit of being married, many church leaders feel it is more relevant to make a stand on the issue. As a result, they make rules about it. Most would say that living together, sharing a life, having sex and/or children, setting up household, and living as if you are married when you are not, is sinful. It's not just a matter of a disagreement of opinion; much of the church sees it as displeasing before God. For this reason, a leader with this view cannot place anyone in leadership when they know one is in such a relationship. Thus, couples are required to be legally married before the church welcomes them for service.

Many leaders assume such a position is implied. As a result, they often don't make this position clear when people volunteer for church service. It would probably benefit most people seeking leadership positions if church leaders held interest meetings to explain things before anyone offers. Criteria for service should always be clear and never hidden to pop up later in time. I would also encourage you to pray about whatever it is you feel called to do, so when the time comes, you know where you should be.

What I would tell you to do is to pray and talk with your leader about the issues you have in your relationship. Ask your leader to support you in prayer as you come to discover what is best for you: not what might look right on paper, but what is best for you, as a person, to do for yourself. Your pastor's concerns are for the house of God and the example that needs to be set for everyone in church, but you have needs as a person. Those need to be examined before venturing into further service. If you know your pastor is for you and you trust them, that's where you need to go. If that's not the case, you need to talk to someone else to help you discern these issues. Know in the long run, the best thing you can do is what is right for you, because that will open the door for you to discover a whole new world of blessings and promises.

How do I Politely Tell People That I Don't Want to Have Any Kids?

I don't know if there is a polite way to tell someone else something isn't their business, but I'll try!

Most people in this world marry and have at least one child. It's what's expected; it is considered the "next" stage in someone's life; it is, in many cultures, deemed a necessity for social and financial reasons; and it is, by many, considered a great joy and blessing in one's life. Some people credit having children as the best thing to ever happen to them, offering maturity and important growth in their human experience.

This is not the case for everyone, no matter how many people hope – and assume – it will be. There are those who describe parenting as a stressful, difficult experience. I have met quite a few parents who, if they had it to do over again, wouldn't have any children at all. The expense, the stress, the feeling like you are never able to do anything but take care of children, the constant disruptions to one's life and marriage, and the difficulties of navigating parenthood definitively turn some parents off to the experience indefinitely.

Those who often ask this question also don't consider those couples who can't have children, and that people deal with such different ways. It's not exactly something that most feel comfortable sharing with the entire world and are content to say it's something that's not for them. Those who don't let the issue drop and who persist in asking don't ever consider how rude their line of questioning might be, as this is often a sensitive issue for people in that predicament.

The decision about having children is a personal one, although it often doesn't feel that way. Many believe they should have children because it's what they saw all their lives, it is what is expected of them, it will bring about an incredible amount of meaning, or it will somehow complete their lives. These ideas are so prevalent, many believe they are true. You are experiencing the results of idealized parenthood: a world that thinks children are indispensable and not having them means you are missing out on the greatest thing in life.

There's no denying that being a parent is an awesome experience for many people. However, having children is simply not for everyone. It is your decision as to whether it's for you. If others don't understand this is how you feel, then it is unfortunately something they will not understand.

I have done extensive teaching over the years on the "barren woman" of Scripture and why this woman is specifically spoken of as being "blessed." The Bible teaches us that having children is its own reward, but the barren woman (or the woman who has no children) is specifically spoken of as being "blessed." While having children is its own reward, the childless woman has room to be filled by something else in her life – the work and Spirit of God. In that place, she is truly free. Unbound by the requirements, financial burdens, and sacrifices of childcare, the childless woman is free to explore the work of God and the world without the confines of being a parent, which limit and ground life experience, at minimum, until children are grown.

Even though the study I did was gender-specific, the concept of "barrenness" can apply to anyone. Everyone experiences the period of "the barren woman" at some point in their lives, whether due to singleness, childlessness, menopause, or empty nest. Some experience it longer than others or more long-term, and for that reason, everyone should understand the idea of its freedom, even if it's hard to fathom long-term.

It is perfectly acceptable to tell others this isn't their life, it is not their choice, and while you appreciate their interest and concern, this isn't a topic you desire to discuss with them. However much you decide to offer beyond this is your choice, but you are perfectly within your right to tell others that you do not desire to discuss such a personal decision with them. It's fine to be blessed, to be free, and to celebrate that – just as much as someone celebrates the birth of a baby or being a parent.

I'VE SEEN DISCUSSIONS ON SOCIAL MEDIA DESCRIBING MEN AS "PRIESTS" AND "KINGS." ARE WOMEN "PRIESTESSES" AND A "QUEENS"?

If you pay careful attention to those discussions, there is probably one notable factor in every single one of them. They talk about men as the priests and kings of their homes, they reiterate it's all a huge responsibility, and how men need to have women behind them for that huge task. Every now and then you will hear talk women as queens, but never a priestess. Think over these conversations; in all that is stated, what is missing?

The answer: there is never a single Biblical passage or verse offered in support of the viewpoint. It's something taught, echoed, and believed, but no one ever has any Scriptural support for it. The reason for why is simple: there isn't any.

The Scriptures provide for two types of priests: the Levitical priesthood of the Old Testament and the priesthood of all believers in the New Testament. The Old Testament Levitical priesthood consisted of men from the tribe of Levi who served as leaders in the tabernacle and temple of old, offering the various sacrifices required for the remission of sin. They stood in the gap between God the Israelites. After Christ's death on the cross, the Levitical priesthood was no longer necessary, and church leadership took a different posture and purpose. According to the New Covenant, all believers are a "royal priesthood," meaning we have been set apart by God for to do His work in this world. While we are not mediators in the sense that Christ is a mediator, we are those appointed to bring people back to God while we are on this earth.

No one ever understood the priesthood to be something done within the home. It was an acceptable and important service to the nation of Israel, a public work. Now in the context of the priesthood of all believers, it is a service we, as the Body of Christ, render to the world. There is no such thing as a "priest of the home." Such a limitation is in contradiction to the priesthood of the believers and the work we are called to do.

The word "priestess" is seldom used because it was associated with pagan identity and pagan rite. A we are one in Christ, the preferential gender-inclusive term (priesthood reflecting a group that is inclusive of all people) was associated with male usage. It's not that women are not included, but that with a group identity, it's understood it includes everyone.

To say any of us in Christianity are "kings" or "queens" when we are not a part of an earthly royal office denotes a ruling authority contrary to the Biblical commands that we are to submit one to another and not esteem ourselves more highly than we should. Identifying oneself in such a way would have never, ever been considered in Protestant times, if for no other reason than the monarchs of old were considered corrupt, indecent, and contrary to Christianity. Their laws and governances were often the result of political ties with state churches. As believers, we should be satisfied with the identities we have in Christ, and we should promote values of humility, honesty, and truth instead of trying to raise one another up to monarchy-like standards. Every one of us needs to learn how to operate as the servants of the King – Jesus Christ – rather than trying to raise ourselves up to an equivalent level. Instead of worrying about these weird identities that people make up, be who you are and who God has called you – and let the rest work the same out for themselves.

MY FRIENDS ALWAYS HAVE SO MUCH ADVICE FOR ME ON WHAT I SHOULD DO NEXT, BUT I'M NOT SURE. WHOSE ADVICE SHOULD I FOLLOW?

Friends are one of the best parts of life. It's an awesome feeling to connect with someone and find the support, information, and encouragement we need. It's awesome to know we can offer the same to someone else and to find that mutual symbiotic relationship in friendship. We don't often find that kind of closeness and connection with family members or siblings, so friends supply an important world outlook for us and an important encouragement, especially in our faith.

Friends can be an essential component when it is time to step out, do something new, or when we need advice or prayer. This doesn't always mean that friends, no matter how well-intentioned, always steer us in the right direction. The more friends we have, the greater variety of different opinions we find, especially if our friends are on different spiritual levels. As much as we might love our friends, it doesn't mean our friends always know what is best for us.

If you aren't sure about the advice your friends give you, you need to wait it out a bit and take some discernment time to sort matters out for yourself. Sometimes people give us advice from different places and perspectives. We don't need to only consider the advice we get, but what we feel led to do. It might be to do what your friends suggest, what one friend suggests, or what none of your friends suggest. What is right for us isn't always as clear to others as it is to us, and that means we must consider all options to make sure what we do is right.

In a larger sense, you also need to take some time and

seek God's direction on the matters at hand. What God advises considers all things, including things our friends don't (such as unforeseeable changes). His manner of direction never fails or misleads us. Our friends mean well, but God knows well! God's divine direction will never veer us off course.

The advice you should follow is from God. If this means if God is speaking through one or more of your friends, great; if not, then pursue God for His word to you. Unless there's some sort of spiritual push, there is no reason to feel pressured. Take your time before moving forward and seek the face of God for your need. If these people are truly your friends, they want what's best for you even if it's not what they recommend. Friends will support your process and give you the time and space to figure out what is right for you at this time in your life.

Isn't a Woman's Place in the Home?

One of my favorite memes features a large group, presumably a women's march from the 1960s, with a box across the center that says, "A woman's place is everywhere." I feel it echoes truth that is in contrast with what we often hear as women. Even though it may not be a popular truth or an overwhelming truth, the facts are the facts: a woman's place is everywhere. Anywhere a woman is called to be, that is her place. As a result, women should be encouraged to discover wherever they find their place this side of heaven.

What this means: nobody, and I mean nobody, has the right to tell a woman she has a perceived "place." Nobody is saying a woman shouldn't handle responsibilities but should suit her responsibilities to wherever she is supposed to be. It isn't someone else's place to tell a woman she belongs somewhere specific, is only able to do certain things, or can only achieve so much, on account of gender.

We can thank the Victorian Era of history for "gender norms" as we understand them today. It was Queen Victoria who established the idea that women should not enter the worldly sphere. Such was seen as unladylike and undignified for society women. Men were considered able-minded and bodied enough to handle the rigors of the outside world. Thus, we see the standards of "gender roles" as we often understand them today. This concept, however, was an ideal set for women of a certain social standing. Such was never an attainment for women who had to work, usually in low-paying jobs or even as slaves, because they were not part of a high enough social class. They didn't have the convenience of no longer working and living off their husbands' incomes.

When a woman had to work, she was looked down on as having a lesser societal status than women who didn't have to work.

If we fast-forward to the 1920s, 1940s, and then beyond, women have consistently fought to work outside the home. Over time, the understanding that women should be in the home, working for free, became demoralizing. Women were seen as less than men, their work was seen as less valuable, and it was understood that women weren't good for or competent for anything else. As a result, women rose up, fought, and in many places in the world, continue to fight for their rights as citizens and workers.

The real fight, however, was for women to make their own choice about their lives, their place, and their futures. It wasn't to dictate what those choices, places, and futures were; it was to give women a sense of freedom to find their own paths. Every woman is different, we have different combinations of gifts and abilities, and we shouldn't feel limited to certain spheres, whether dictated by culture, church, or anyone in what we are able to do or pursue in our lives.

That having been said: this means women have the responsibility (the decision to seek God's will) to discover the right place for us. It isn't specifically in the home, or the boardroom, or even as a minister of a church, unless that's where we are supposed to be. It is anywhere that God directs.

It's perfectly fine to be a stay-at-home mom or homemaker if that is where you feel called to be. There's nothing wrong with it. It's not a demotion. If your call is to be at home and take care of your kids, family, household, and that is your exclusive focus, that's awesome. You should be celebrated for the commitment you've made.

It's perfectly fine to be a businesswoman or careerwoman

and to focus on that in your life, without being much of a homebody. Some people aren't much for cooking and cleaning or more domestic hobbies. It doesn't make you bad, it doesn't make you unfulfilled, it doesn't mean you are missing anything. It just means you find your place, your contentment and sense of satisfaction in a different place than someone else. If that's where you are to be, then go for it!

It's perfectly fine to be a combination of both a wife and/or mother and a professional. It might take some balancing, but it's fine to do both if that is where you know you are equipped and called to be.

It's also perfectly fine to be in ministry and any combination of the circumstances above. No matter what you are called to do, it's where you are best suited to be.

Also recognize it is perfectly acceptable to be somewhere for a while and find it isn't your place anymore or that you have outgrown it. It's fine to change the place where you are, keeping in mind each and every responsibility you have in your situations. Your place might change, and that's all right, too.

So no, a woman's place is not specifically in the home or specifically anywhere else, for that matter. It is for her to respond and answer wherever she is called. Just as the women in the Bible answered different calls: Military leadership, household management, preaching, working as businesswomen, operating home-based businesses, being mothers, serving in the five-fold, taking care of widows, making clothes, leading in song, and beyond, we are able to see that God has many, many different places – and purposes – for His women.

I'M NOT COMFORTABLE WITH WHAT IS GOING ON IN OUR SCHOOLS TODAY. SHOULD I CONSIDER HOME-SCHOOLING MY CHILDREN?

I am not sure what side of the debate you are on, but there is no question our schools have become a ridiculous political battleground with students in the middle. It's not possible for the endless policies, changes, and debates to not impact students in a negative way. Such impacts learning, the school atmosphere, the quality of teaching, and the general feelings of tension between students and teachers and teachers and staff. School has become something other than what it was created to be, and it's not hard to imagine why you might desire to take your kids out of the mire and see to their education yourselves.

There are a few things to consider before making the plunge to home-schooling. The first is your own motive for doing so. Are you worried about your kids making you look bad as a parent, falling in with a bad crowd, about bad influences, rebelling, or is it something else? As a parent it can be hard to accept, but kids need to learn to both test boundaries and learn from them. Trying to isolate your kids from the general population in the hopes they will keep in tow might seem like a good idea, but it keeps them from developing their own sense of personal responsibility, especially if they are used to going to school. This may very well not be your motive, but it is something to think about, especially if your children are in their teenage years and their behavior is a motivating factor. It's easy to blame it on what they are being taught when it might be nothing more than normal teenage rebellion as they try to assert themselves. I recognize this doesn't necessarily look good and it is different from behavior that causes concern (such as teenage sex or drug use) but if it's falling within the normal boundaries, it's something to roll with and handle as it comes along rather than disrupting their entire lives.

Beyond this consideration, home-schooling falls within certain legalities that parents must abide by to continue educating their children at home. Textbooks must fall within certain accepted standards; parents must file reports a few times per year with their county school districts proving the student is continuing in academic studies and must complete annual standardized testing (either at a private or public school) to prove students keep up with academic standards. It's not as simple as deciding you want to educate your child as you see fit, as children must still receive education within the standards required by law.

This means home-schooling families must take the time to familiarize themselves with the requirements at hand and figure out how they will rise to meet them. Students must also adhere to a disciplined day, with a schedule much like they already have at school, to complete their assignments, tasks, homework, and projects on a regularly scheduled basis. Parents need to have the knowledge of subjects at hand to help when problems arise, grade papers, enforce educational standards, and help children structure their days and learn their assigned subjects. In other words, home-schooling is a time-consuming project, something that requires parents are involved with their children's education in a very demanding way, and it is not something that can just be done as one goes along, because it won't work well.

Home-schooled children also need to be involved in different social projects with kids their own age, whether they are other home-schooled children, sports, social activities, church activities, community involvement, and other ways they can develop important social skills and interactions with their peers. In some school districts, home-schooled children are allowed to use school facilities such as the library or allow them to participate in drama or band, but this does depend on where you live.

If you are concerned about your children's education, there are other options besides traditional home-schooling. One is a home-schooling cooperative, consisting of groups of families who also home-school and assist each other in educating and socializing their children. Another option is private school, such as a Catholic school or Christian school. My only advice with Christian schooling is to carefully examine academic standards and curriculum, to make sure they meet state standards for educational excellence rather than propaganda.

I would encourage you to sincerely pray and seek God about your best course of action, exploring options to discover what is best for your children, your family, and your situation. Also, if you have different resources available to you, such as a home-schooling family or cooperative, talk to some different people about what the experience is like, so you can determine what will be best for all of you.

My Daughter is Gay.
What Do I Do About This?

You love her and treat her with the same respect and love that you did before she trusted you enough to come out to you.

I understand church culture has not always been particularly inviting to the LGBTQ+ community and their families. I know judgment comes when you have a daughter who identifies as a lesbian, and that some people may regard your faith in a specific light on account of that. I am saying this to acknowledge I recognize the pressures that exist, and I understand that, combined with much of what is often said in church about LGBTQ+ individuals can make you feel as if your daughter's sexual orientation is somehow a stab against you, a statement against God, and something that is the worst of the worst. None of this is true, but as such circulates, it can make you feel your daughter has a terrible, unspeakable flaw, and you must do something to fix it.

I've spent many years working within the LGBTQ+ community and their families, and I can say with assurance that no parent, anywhere on this earth, does anything to "make" their children gay. Science doesn't understand attraction in partners of the opposite sex, let alone understanding it with those of the same sex. All the rhetoric you hear that being gay is a choice, something that can be fixed with behavior modification, that people who are gay should be abandoned or isolated from their families, or that being LGBTQ+ can be "fixed" by outside pressures or conditioning are long-held myths that hurt everyone in these situations. Because the church is unprepared and unwilling to handle these issues in a better way, such drives people in these situations to find new churches or belief systems, wind up isolated and disconnected from their families, and hurt and alienated.

Whether or not you are a part of a denomination opposed to gay marriage or homosexual relationships, no one can deny that before these issues became political, no one talked about them. If someone was gay, no one spoke much about it. No one assumed someone else's orientation. Nowadays, the topic is all over church, with people making judgments and accusations without facts. Let's understand there is no "spirit of homosexuality." It doesn't exist within Scripture, and there is nothing to indicate the ancients thought such a thing existed. There is also some question as to Biblical context for the few references it appears to make about same-sex sexual situations (not all of them are about that) thanks to bad translations over the past forty or fifty years. But no matter what has changed in church or what has changed in the overall attitude and consensus toward the LGBTQ+ community, it remains constant that Scripture commands us to love others. Loving others demands a certain posture from believers. Even if you don't agree with your daughter's orientation on principle you can still love your daughter, have her in your life, and share with her, just as you would in any other situation. I'm sure there are many things the two of you probably disagree about, but because she is your daughter, you don't break your relationship with her because of them. This is no different; she is still your daughter, and you still want to have her in your life, and she wants to have you in hers. Continue to be there for her, support her, celebrate her life milestones, and move toward a healthy, solid, adult relationship with her.

I would also encourage you to seek out some resources on this issue to help you to better understand the realities about sexual orientation and learn more about what Scripture teaches on this topic. It might be difficult to navigate and even accept at first, but the sense of freedom you will find in discovering all is not lost for daughter and she is not hated by God will empower you.

Don't concern yourself so much with what others might think or feel about this issue. This is your daughter, and you have to feel free to care about, love, and spend time with your daughter, no matter who – or what – has a problem with it. In someone's eyes, you will always do the wrong thing, but there is no way you can go wrong in your relationship with your daughter by loving her.

ARE THINGS LIKE ORAL SEX AND MASTURBATION SINFUL?

A question angled and debated over the years, the issues of both oral sex and masturbation are often seen as controversial. These are private matters and shouldn't be ones so quickly up for debate about people's personal lives. No matter how one sees it, it's not a discussion that should be up for debate involving an entire church community or the internet.

To start with the latter, the Bible doesn't hold a specific position on masturbation. It, in fact, does not mention it at all. The most we find mention of is in the specifically male context of possible "emissions," mentioned in the Old Covenant. Leviticus 15:16 specifically mentions such without the possibility of partnered sexual relations:

When a man has an emission of semen, he must bathe his whole body with water, and he will be unclean till evening.

The context of this passage – whether in regard to masturbation or any physical emission – is not clarified. The general nature of the statement tells us it is about any physical release because such would have been a hygiene issue. Long before people in this world knew about things such as DNA evidence or disease contamination, the hygiene rules present in Scripture let everyone know disease could spread through such fluids. This is why washing and "separation" were required when such discharges occurred. To have such a release wasn't sinful in and of itself, but since disease or contamination could occur, the rules existed for that reason.

There is no specified passage as relates to women. Every Biblical passage as pertains to women and uncleanness relates to period blood or "discharge." There were all sorts of rules and regulations about what women could or couldn't do while on their periods, but there is no other specific context as pertains to women. Thus, we could say the same applies: these were matters of hygiene rather than morality, and their application today is understood in that light, rather than in one of moral context. There aren't any Biblical verses that prohibit masturbation, which can be done for many reasons.

As for oral sex, there are passages that do mention such in Scripture. It is often spoken in a metaphorical or coded language, but our knowledge of language usage and custom does confirm these passages are a reference to such. Perhaps the best known is Song of Solomon 2:3-6:

Like an apple tree among the trees of the forest
*   is my beloved among the young men.*
I delight to sit in his shade,
*   and his fruit is sweet to my taste.*
Let him lead me to the banquet hall,
*   and let his banner over me be love.*
Strengthen me with raisins,
*   refresh me with apples,*
*   for I am faint with love.*
His left arm is under my head,
*   and his right arm embraces me.*

The individual speaking in this passage is the woman. That isn't to say such sexual practices should be one-sided, but that there is a healthy, normal view of sexual relationships on the part of the woman. She didn't try to sweep her feelings and desires under the rug, pretending they weren't there. She wasn't coy or shy, but open about what she enjoyed doing and wanted to do with her mate. There was no shame in their intimate relationship. That tells us what people do in their intimate lives is their business, and we have no right to shame them for it.

Any matters that relate to sex are controversial because sex is often seen as taboo, problematic, or sinful. There is nothing in Scripture that states sex is bad. There are examples of sex used in aggression, as a weapon, or improperly exercised, but there is nothing that says all sex is bad. Unless we live with someone in an arrangement that specifies sex is off the table (such as when one is asexual or someone has a medical condition that prevents sex), we can't expect our relationship to find its proper balance and purpose without embracing the sexual part of one's being. If we forever feel we are doing something bad, we will find ourselves ashamed of something when we have no reason to do so.

When it comes to sexual interests, they are a matter of personal preference. Consent is essential. Otherwise, couples should discuss their likes and dislikes and therefore decide together what they would like to do, explore, and discover about each other. It is my best advice to say leave the church out of these issues. A vote, an opinion, or a long-winded lecture on behalf of another is not necessary. Feel confident in this most intimate part of your life, and as always, communicate with your partner.

What is "Normal?"

Everywhere you look it seems like this question plagues the minds of many people. What is "normal?" What is a "normal" life? What is a "normal" Christian? What is a "normal" marriage? There are many who would attempt to answer this question, all of which have their own arsenal of answers as to what "normal" is. Who is right?

There is the context of "normal" as something we do, or pursue, or handle, that is within the range of personal benefit, health, or sanity. In other words: if you are hoarding items because you feel doing so is for some greater good, then what you are doing could be described as outside the range of "normal." Hoarding isn't good for one's mental health, benefit, or sanity. In such an instance, we could say the behavior is out of the realm of "normal." It doesn't mean someone is bad, just that someone needs help. Getting that help means such an individual can reach a place of "normal" in their lives, where things are not so difficult or strenuous.

Defining "normal," however doesn't mean we have to conform to an abstract set of criteria for the things we do in our lives. If we are living lives of personal benefit, health, and sanity, and is in no way a threat or harm to others, our lives and our "normal" is not going to look the same as someone else's. What we do isn't abnormal; it is simply different. We know God allows for differences: gifts, abilities, talents, etc., and as we explore such, we are better able to find the "normal" God has for each one of us.

Should Christians Smoke Weed?

It seems like anywhere you turn, there is always an advocate for either the medicinal or recreational use of marijuana – or sometimes both. Those who advocate for the use of marijuana often claim it to be a cure-all for just about everything imaginable: the stimulation of hair growth, pain management, curing nausea or hangovers, correcting seizures or mental illness, and all while providing a buzz to users.

If you are anything like me, you probably wonder how much the claims to marijuana's medical benefits are true. The truth is, there isn't much evidence to bespeak its use as a cure-all. It has been known to benefit certain seizure disorders as well as nausea in chemotherapy patients, but there is little to no evidence to support its use for other things. Those who use it independently, without medical supervision, are not part of controlled studies and benefit from a high more than medically supported documentation. Without ample evidence, the debate about weed rages on – and Christians wonder, where should we stand on the issue.

In defense of drug use, there have been several theories about the recreational or sometimes self-described "sacramental" use of marijuana in the Bible. Despite different theories, there is no mention of marijuana in the Bible and definitively no evidence to say it was ever used as part of Old Testament rites. While yes, it is safe to say it is a natural plant and God did create everything, God did not intend all plants to be ingested. For example, poison ivy is also a natural part of creation, but that doesn't mean it's wise to smoke it. Also, given we live in the world after the fall of mankind, not all plants function or survive as they did before the fall – and that means they may also have different side effects or purposes than they had prior.

There are a few passages cited, namely Exodus 30:23, Isaiah 18:4-5, Ezekiel 34:29, and Revelation 22:1-2 in defense of its use. It's worth noting that marijuana, hemp, and cannabis are not specifically mentioned anywhere in these passages, and there is no evidence to suggest their interpretation in the passages through translation. The most commonly invoked passage is Exodus 30:23:

Take the following fine spices: 500 shekels of liquid myrrh, half as much (that is, 250 shekels) of fragrant cinnamon, 250 shekels of fragrant calamus...

This passage details the preparation for holy anointing oil, used for Levitical ceremonies. In some older translations, the term "fragrant calamus" is translated "sweet cane." The Hebrew for this term is *qenêh-bośem,* which literally refers to a "sweet water-plant" or "sweet grain." It is definitely not a reference to marijuana but is most likely calamus – a plant native to India that was widely believed to have medicinal properties. Even if it was a reference to marijuana (it's not), this passage does not ever state such usage included smoking or ingestion of any sort.

Hemp was widely known throughout the Middle East for its practical use: rope, textiles, oil, incense, and in edible seed form. Israel's pagan nations also possibly used it as part of magic rites (along with other intoxicants) to induce trances or sleep states. For this reason alone, its use would not have been part of Israel's ceremonial life, simply because they were forbidden to practice magic.

In modern times, the verdict on medicinal use of weed is

still out. While I believe controlled use under a doctor's care for management of specified conditions does have value, there is no justification for recreational use. The use of secondary products, such as cannabidiol (CBD) and Delta-8 are also sketchy, with no evidence to back their over-the-counter cure-all claims. Both also come with potential side effects and as they are sold as "supplements," their contents are not evaluated for safety by governing agencies. If we are to apply Biblical wisdom, the Bible does state being "intoxicated," or in an altered state due to a substance (such as being high or stoned) is contrary to Biblical injunction. Given there is no other recreational purpose for the use of marijuana other than intoxication, its recreational use is not supported by Scripture.

What is the Bible's Approach to Dating a Non-Believer?

In my many years of Christian faith, I have attended many churches that prohibited dating, marrying, or having anything to do with someone deemed a "non-believer." In some, we were prohibited from having friends who were not believers let alone dating someone who wasn't classified as a Christian. We were often told "light has no fellowship with darkness" and dating a non-believer was paramount to retreating to the dark side, backsliding, and failing in one's faith, and all these ideas and concepts are found in the Bible. But...are they?

In Old Testament times, the Israelites weren't just a spiritual entity. They were also a nation, a race, a literal group of people trying to survive amidst occupations, overthrows, and neighbors that sometimes got too close. The Biblical prohibitions on inter-tribal marriage existed for the preservation of the Israelites, but it wasn't so much about racial preservation as that of spiritual tradition. The Israelites had an entire law, custom, culture, and belief system that varied from their neighbors. If they wanted to continue, they needed to make sure they practiced self-preservation. It couldn't be preserved if they married someone of another tribe and started worshiping their gods, engaging in their practices, and forsaking their own. The Israelites weren't good at holding resolve when it came to the spiritual practices of their neighbors, and that meant in a marital situation, they would be quick to lose their identity.

This becomes even more relevant when we recognize marriage in ancient times was as much about alliances and tribal agreements as it was about a couple's relationship. As I stated earlier, ancient marriages were about forging connections between different groups. If the Israelites were seeking to forge an alliance, it was, most likely, going to involve spiritual adjustments. Since ancient relationships were about far more than just getting to know a person, interfaith marriage was prohibitive.

It is important to note, however, that such prohibitions weren't on couples as a rule (unless a man was leaving his spouse to pursue a foreign wife). They were on the families who arranged marriages for their children, as was the custom in ancient times. There was no dating because marriages were arranged. The responsibility of seeing that marriage remained within Israel's boundaries belonged to the parents or guardians of a family – not the couple themselves. If we fast-forward to New Testament times, we do not see such relationships as entirely prohibitive, but an encouragement for interfaith marriages to continue as long as there was no other substantial reason to separate. Instead of feeling such would cause a believing spouse to stray, it was believed that a Christian spouse may have the ability to influence their non-believing spouse.

Since the Bible doesn't embrace nor teach anything about dating, there isn't anything specific in the Bible about dating a non-believer. There are a few things I would say though, to keep in mind. While such is not entirely prohibitive, there are obvious reasons why such could become complicated. It's good to be prepared when questions or discussions arise. It's good to know where your potential partner comes from as far as their own beliefs are concerned, and what they prefer or find personally prohibitive. It's great to have conversations and not feel like your faith is off limits, even if they don't share it with you. Communication becomes key, even as it is in any relationship

The major negative of dating someone who doesn't share your faith is that they do not share your faith. You may have major differences of opinion about important life issues. Religion has a way of shaping how people see the world, intimate relationships, marriage, dating, and family life. You may disagree about how to spend your time or finances, family disciplines and disagreements, intimate arrangements, and what you desire to do with your life or how you live in general. Only you can decide if these differences are to be overcome. The decision as to do this – or not do this – often relates to your intentions for the relationship. Some relationships are casual and fun without the anticipation of marriage or long-term commitment. If your dating experience is about an event or a few times to have fun, it may not be as much of an issue as if you are seeking marriage.

I also want to add I don't recommend deliberately dating someone because they are a non-believer. While such might seem like a great way to evangelize, it has a way of falling apart if that's your motive. We should never, ever use dating as a means of evangelization, in the hopes someone will come around to our way of thinking or believing if they decide they can't live without us. Such can make someone feel manipulated, deceived, or plain angry. When the Bible talks about the character of a believing spouse winning over an unbelieving one, it isn't talking about a manipulative attempt to get someone to convert through a relationship. Rather, the advice is such so that without trying, Christian character is lived. Such is seen by others, including their spouse. It's not about some sort of secret mission to convert or fix someone, but about the ability to see the fruit of your walk in your relationship.

If you are interested in dating an unbeliever with intent to marry, you need to see your relationship through, even if that individual never converts. It can't be a relationship hinging on a potential or possible conversion. Rather, you love and embrace that person for who they are. If you can't do this, it is better you wait – and prepare – yourself to date someone else later in time.

How Do I Know the Will of God for My Life?

Ah, the will of God. Something that seems mysterious and compounding at the same time. Whenever we are faced with a choice, we are reminded about how important it is to be in God's will. The bigger the choice, the more essential it is we follow "God's will." We see the will of God as a narrow binary: something we are either in or out. If we are not in the will of God, we will miss all the opportunities and options that will make our lives worthwhile. The entirety of God's will hinges on singular decisions, or so it would sound.

It sounds punitive. It's a massive amount of pressure. It sounds like every decision we make turns into a crisis: chose this or that with the blessings of God awaiting on one end, and the torment of trouble on the other. Which way do we choose? Which way is obvious? Maybe the bigger question is, which way will I find God?

The will of God and how we discern the will of God has been discussed for centuries. I don't think there has been any singular consensus about the will of God or how to know for certain we are in the will of God. Discovering God's will for our lives is a deep and personal process, one that unfolds throughout time and changes as we grow in our faith. It is God's will that we develop a better sense of His presence in our lives, no matter what our circumstances may be. I also believe that, regardless of the results of our decisions, it is God's will that we find Him in those situations.

When we talk about discerning the will of God, we aren't trying to understand God's will in situations. What we are often trying to do is hope our faith can guide us to make decisions that will be consequence-free. The ultimate goal is to make our interpretation of God's will a tangible thing rather than something that is often abstract and hard-to-discern. We think if we pray enough and hope hard enough, we can have a life different than the one we have. It's a nice idea and a great theory, but if you live long enough and dive into spiritual depths long enough, you will find this method often doesn't work.

We pray and seek God, believing a situation is completely within His will, and then we get to the other side of it to discover it has consequences. Maybe our friends or family don't understand it. Everything is going wrong with the project. We hit numerous walls. Every time things start to get better, they get worse again soon after. Then we sit back and start to wonder about our choices. Should we have chosen something else? Did we "miss" God?

We like the idea of being able to foretell the future and see great things from the outset, not anticipating that life happens no matter what choices we make. We also like the idea of making every decision we make a moral one; in other words, we place an excessive amount of weight on them, sometimes giving things permanence they may not have. The idea of changing courses makes us uncomfortable, and we like to think decisions are etched in life, fixed, and immovable, no matter what might come along.

The truth about decisions is that we make them all the time. Every choice we make is a decision, even if we don't take time to ponder and consider the results. Our lives are not just the product of the big decisions we face, but the product of smaller decisions, the responses of others to our decisions, and sometimes the fact that fate, as we might call it, has different plans from ours. In our decision-making, we are there to learn from mistakes, make different choices, and accept that sometimes life does exactly what life is going to do, no matter what we do.

The first thing we need to understand is the will of God isn't always clear in situations because it's not supposed to be. The Bible tells us that we see spiritual things as through a reflection:

For now we see only a reflection as in a mirror; then we shall see face to face. Now I know in part; then I shall know fully, even as I am fully known. (1 Corinthians 13:12)

Some theologians wonder why this is; I believe it both forces us to have faith and to rely on God rather than spiritual gifts or abilities. God not only gives us the ability to make our own decisions; He encourages it. Free will is an essential to the Christian walk; we must follow God of our own choosing. God gives us choices, and He honors our choices.

That fact, right there, is a game changer when it comes to the will of God. Knowing God honors our choices gives us a different perspective on making them all together. God is already in the future. He knows the choices we will make before we make them. If He knows our choices, He has anticipated and made room for them. His plan doesn't come about with an abstract sense of His will, but in considering both His will and our choices and movements throughout life. It's a mutual work, one by which we partner with God as He brings us to a deeper sense of who we are and how to understand what is best for us. The better we understand who we are called to be, the better sense we have of God in our situations, no matter the outcome.

This doesn't mean decisions can't be "right" or "wrong," but it does mean most choices are a lot more complicated than any one set of singular results. It's not as simple to judge them through such a limited lens. It also doesn't mean that decision-making isn't complicated. Recognizing this, how do we make the best choices possible? There are a few things to keep in mind when it comes to decision-making, especially when considering the will of God in any situation:

- Not every decision we face – even big ones – are moral decisions. They don't all relate to sin, salvation, right, or wrong (in an eternal perspective). Some decisions are just decisions; they are just choices we make. Everything we decide does not have heavy, moral weight on them. For example: deciding to move to a new city or take a new job are not moral decisions. While they might have some sort of moral implication with them at some point (such as being faced with a moral dilemma on the job), that is not necessarily related to deciding to take the job itself.

- It's perfectly possible that a decision is right in the immediate but won't be forever. Just because a decision is right for right now doesn't mean it has to still stand several years in the future.

- Encountering opposition doesn't mean God isn't in the decision you made. Consequence-free decision making doesn't exist, but we are given the impression that if we seek God, situations won't have obstacles, difficulties, or consequences. This is a misnomer. Decisions always have consequences, no matter what we choose. It is perfectly possible to encounter opposition or difficulty in a situation and God still be there, in it, teaching you something essential and important. We cannot decide a decision is right or wrong based on difficulties we may encounter. No matter which choice you make, difficulties will follow; they will just be different difficulties.

- It's possible that situations don't always have obvious choices or good choices. You can be faced with two – or more – equally difficult decisions, each with their own unique weight and challenge. There may not be a "good option" or even a "best option" all the time. These situations don't mean we are out of God's will but experiencing life and the reality that we are called to seek God's presence, no matter how difficult our circumstances might be.

- The will of God is difficult to discern in foresight is because God's lessons are often had in hindsight. We must go through the ins and outs of a situation before we understand what God is teaching us within it. This is why details of situations often seem different when a situation is past versus when we are in the throes of it. It is also why we are often not rescued from the consequences of our actions.

These different realities reveal to us the essence of decisions and the will of God: life isn't easy. We don't see the end from the beginning, and there isn't always one singular way to remain in the will of God in every situation. We need to mature enough in our faith to find God in every situation we face, whether things turn out the way we desire, or not. No matter what choices we make, God is with us. While deliberately choosing sin will draw us from God, most of our decisions don't have this much impact on our lives. God wants us to know Him in the good and the bad, and ultimately, know His will resides wherever He is.

Is there only one person out there for me? If so, where are they?

One thing I strongly dislike about the modern church's approach to relationships is their exclusivity. I do not mean they are exclusive in a monogamous sense, but they are exclusive in an elimination sense. We are given the message that God has created only one specific person for us; we must wait for this person to appear in our lives to be complete; this person will be a perfect complement to us, in every way; we will have no conflicts; and this person will be everything we need.

I believe people give this message to keep single people on the straight and narrow. They don't want single people dating multiple people to be tempted toward "worldly ways" of living together or sex outside of marriage. The only problem with this message is that being single is hard. If you've been single for any length of time, it's easy to feel discouraged, as if things will never happen for you.

In my own experience, so many people said this to me that it made me feel hopeless. There are more than seven billion people in the world. Trying to find some mystery perfect "one" felt like looking for a needle in a haystack. It felt intimidating. If anything, it felt cruel. If there is some "perfect person," why aren't they right in front of us? Why aren't they easy to find? It felt like a cosmic, crazy joke.

We need to step back and first accept the concept of one perfect person; one "soulmate" isn't a real thing. It's something concocted in fairy tales that end with "and they lived happily ever after." That singular phrase leaves us to conjure images of a perfect life in our heads, without consideration to just what married life, spiritual life, coupled life is like with another person. When we spend all our time looking for "one," what we are really hoping for is that happy ending perfect life image, one that will be conflict free and give us the perceived freedom to be who we are without any confinements.

The second thing we need to accept: relationships of any sort are choices we make. We make decisions about who is right for us based on what we seek in a mate and how we best want to live our lives with someone else. We don't decide to be in relationship with someone because they fall out of the sky on our car. Our decision to be in a long-term relationship with someone comes because they have certain attributes and characteristics that we desire. We see ourselves as both a compliment to them and a fulfillment of the different needs we have. It's a delicate balance that isn't always 100%, nor is it all one way or the other.

Third: all relationships matter. Focusing so much on finding a spouse is unhealthy, at least in my opinion. We have family members, friends, and "found family" members who are just as important and relevant in our lives as those who we might date or marry. Community is essential to any functional, healthy relationship; we don't trade off one for another. Having good people in your life makes the journey not just worthwhile but helps diminish loneliness and obsessive tendencies to find "the one." Instead of finding one, you have the honor of finding many people who care about you throughout your life.

Last, it's also important to remember some relationships work, while some do not. Some work for a period of time and then end. Nobody and nothing are perfect this side of heaven. With over seven billion people in the world, a broken relationship doesn't mean the end. It means we take the time we need and then we try again. In the meantime, we spend our time with friends and family, establishing strong foundations so we can enjoy a full life with community rather than exclusivity. So no, there isn't "one" perfect person for you out there. There is one you find who you can see yourself forging the ins and outs, ups and downs of life alongside. You embrace them as much as your communal support system through the various seasons of life.

Was Jesus married to Mary Magdalene?

Holy Blood, Holy Grail. The DaVinci Code. The Knights Templar. Internet videos. What do these four things have in common? They all revolve around promoting a legend that Jesus was married to Mary Magdalene. Often woven into fictional stories that ignite the mystery of secrets, conspiracy, and church collusion, the idea that Jesus was married draws ire from both Christians and the secular world alike. It is a shocking notion, one that seems to go against years of traditional understanding as well as Bible text.

To properly understand the elements of the claim, it's important to understand their origins. The "Holy Grail" legend is one that emerged in medieval literature, particularly that of French and British lore. According to its myth, there is a sacred object somehow directly connected to Jesus Christ, one of invaluable worth. It was originally deemed a stone (identified in some media as the "philosopher's stone"); in the twelfth century, it became interwoven with the legend of the Holy Chalice. After this time, the Holy Grail became known as the cup Jesus used during the Last Supper, then used later by Joseph of Arimathea to catch Jesus' blood during the crucifixion. Later myths included the idea that the Holy Grail is a symbol of forbidden knowledge embraced by secret societies, such as the Knights Templar. Lore states that obtaining the Holy Grail would grant miracles, eternal life, the secrets of life itself, eternal youth, and wisdom. It's best known through the legends of King Arthur as well as fodder in more modern times through *Monty Python and the Holy Grail.*

In the 1970s, three writers: Michael Baigent, Richard

Leigh, and Henry Lincoln devised a scandalous theory about the Holy Grail. Instead of seeing it as an object, they thought it might be the literal bloodline of Jesus. According to this theory, the biological descendants of Jesus Christ were the Merovingians, a French family the Catholic Church sought to destroy. Their legacy was preserved then by a secret group known as the Priory of Sion and later, the Knights Templar and the Cathars. In their specific understanding, Jesus was married to Mary Magdalene and had a family prior to His death. This theory was later incorporated into the book *Holy Blood, Holy Grail* in 1982.

Everything related to the Holy Grail – whether it is the idea of it as a sacred stone or cup, or now a bloodline – is entirely fictional. Monty Python's fictious parody is about as accurate as any other grail legend. There is no evidence to suggest such an object ever existed outside of lore and legend. No group known as the Priory of Sion ever existed. There is no evidence that the Knights Templar or Cathars had any such knowledge or connection to preserve any special bloodline. We have no evidence in early church documents, neither Biblical nor non-canonical, that Jesus was ever married – let alone specifically to Mary Magdalene. Even in ancient texts discovered that were documented by groups deemed heretical (such as Gnosticism), there is no mention of Jesus as married or the founder of a sacred bloodline.

I suppose it's safe to say we don't know for certain if Jesus was ever married or fathered a child, as there is always the possibility such was not documented. I find it difficult to fathom, however, that such a monumental event in His life would have gone unrecorded, especially given the documentation we do have about His life and ministry. At some point, mention of a child or a wife would have popped up, much like mention of other relatives (such as His mother and brothers) did throughout the Gospels. Whether it was because a wedding occurred, a wife or child had a question or came looking for Him, or an immediate or extended family member was sick and needed His attention, there would be something to suggest Jesus had this other life. The fact that there is nothing about it bespeaks to me more evidence He did not have a wife or child than that He did.

I would also argue that Jesus' ministry demanded a great deal of His time and attention. Scripture tells us He had nowhere to lay His head (Matthew 8:20, Luke 9:58) and indicates He traveled a great deal between cities and regions. If He was, as these theories proport a husband and father, He would have been absentee on both points. He would not have cared for His family, rendering them destitute. Neither point is in keeping with His advice in Scripture, whether as such relates to divorce (Matthew 5:31-32, Matthew 19:1-11) or caring for children (Matthew 19:13-14).

I believe there is a lot more evidence to bespeak Jesus was unmarried, aromantic, and asexual than to argue a wild theory that He was married. While yes, marriage was often customary and required in His day, that tells me Jesus would have distanced Himself from custom and pioneered single life for the sake of His ministry and example to others.

People will always believe and embrace the idea of conspiracies, believing the lack of evidence for a thing somehow makes it more credible. The idea of the "Holy Grail" as a sacred bloodline while creating a scandalous relationship between Jesus and Mary Magdalene makes for great fiction. I remember reading *The DaVinci Code* years ago and staying up all night to see what happened, chapter after chapter. It was riveting; engaging; and kept me on the edge of my seat. I also kept in mind it is a novel, a story someone made up based on a theory that others also made up. Fiction does not equate to facts. When it comes to the idea that Jesus was married, there is absolutely no fact to back it up.

Can a Christian have tattoos or piercings?

Both tattooing and piercing are ancient practices from tribal times. Tattooing and piercing were done for several different reasons: tribal identification, self-expression, religious practices, ceremonial rites, slavery, display of wealth, offering, or betrothment, engagement, or marriage. We find record of piercing in Scripture in several different contexts, including betrothment, engagement, ceremonial rite, slavery, and display of wealth:

When the camels had finished drinking, the man took out a gold nose ring weighing a beka and two gold bracelets weighing ten shekels... As soon as he had seen the nose ring, and the bracelets on his sister's arms, and had heard Rebekah tell what the man said to her, he went out to the man and found him standing by the camels near the spring. (Genesis 24:22,30)

So they gave Jacob all the foreign gods they had and the rings in their ears, and Jacob buried them under the oak at Shechem. (Genesis 35:4)

Aaron answered them, "Take off the gold earrings that your wives, your sons and your daughters are wearing, and bring them to me." So all the people took off their earrings and brought them to Aaron. (Exodus 32:2-3)

All who were willing, men and women alike, came and brought gold jewelry of all kinds: brooches, earrings, rings and ornaments. They all presented their gold as a wave offering to the Lord. (Exodus 35:22)

Aaron answered them, "Take off the gold earrings that your wives, your sons and your daughters are wearing, and bring them to me." So all the people took off their earrings and brought them to Aaron. (Numbers 31:50)

… and I put a ring on your nose, earrings on your ears and a beautiful crown on your head. (Ezekiel 16:12)

There is no clear prohibition on piercing in Scripture. It was a common practice, one people easily seen and understood within the context of culture. Even though sometimes the gold jewelry used in piercings might have been used for idolatrous purposes (as in the case of the golden calf), there is no expressed prohibition on piercings or body jewelry.

There is one verse in the Bible that directly mentions tattooing. There are a few that mention tattooing indirectly, which help us to understand the proper context of any expressed prohibition on the practice:

Do not cut your bodies for the dead or put tattoo marks on yourselves. I am the Lord. (Leviticus 19:28)

Later in Scripture, we see different perspectives on tattooing:

Some will say, 'I belong to the Lord';
  others will call themselves by the name of Jacob;
still others will write on their hand, 'The Lord's,'
  and will take the name Israel. (Isaiah 44:5)

On his robe and on His thigh He has this name written: King of Kings and Lord of Lords.
(Revelation 19:16)

These three passages provide three examples of ancient tattooing. The first, found in Leviticus, was associated with funeral rites for the deceased. Such a practice was common among pagan tribes. The practice itself would have been prohibited among Israel as it was associated with idolatry and ancestral worship. It wasn't the tattooing that was the issue, but the reason for it.

But just like creating idols out of gold earrings or body jewelry didn't prohibit piercings, so did not this one tattooing practice prohibit all tattoos. Tattooing was also used as a sign of ownership, sometimes done in the case of slavery or servanthood. In Isaiah 44:5, the "writing" (tattooing) on the signified one belonged to God permanently. In Revelation 19:16, we see Jesus returning to fight in battle with a tattoo on His thigh. Such was a warrior tattoo, one that signified self or tribal identity in battle. In this particular passage, Jesus is the ultimate victor, the King and Lord over every other authority that exists in this realm.

Tattooing as is understood in modern times is devoid of the connection to idolatry and funeral rites, unless it is done somewhere in the world within that context. If we recognize tattooing as part of self-expression and body art, there is nothing Biblically prohibitive about it – or piercing – in a modern context.

Is it all right to go to counseling?

Therapeutic practice originally sought to provide insight and assistance to patients diagnosed with mental illnesses. Over the years, therapeutic practice widened its scope and can be of great value to any individual who seeks better insight into themselves, their history, and their decision-making processes. Some people choose to go to counseling to resolve personal trauma or maintain good mental health while others might want to discuss something specific, become better at what they do, or receive job perspective and advice.

Counseling can serve as a powerful means for both advice and healing. The basic goal of counseling is to see things for what they are and through the process and discover the answers one seeks to improve life's situations. Sometimes counseling is a multi-year or regular endeavor, while others go for a short period of time before finding what they need in the process.

Most people seek out counsel at some point in their lives. Whether it's through a counselor or therapist, in the context of Christian counseling with a pastor, minister, or church leader, a mentor or job adviser, or just talk to their friends or family members for insight, we've all sought out the opinions of others to guide us through a process. There's no Biblical prohibition on such practices, so why do some church leaders take issue with therapy?

The purpose of therapy is a little different than Christian counseling or talking with friends about a situation. Through therapy, one speaks and discusses their issues in a safe place with the expressed goal of helping someone to see their issues for themselves and make their own decisions about matters.

It is guided rather than didactic. Good counselors ask questions to cause a client to think about what they want and how they can better themselves. It's an introspective process that draws out need realizations and changes.

This is part of why some church leaders often disagree with therapy. In their approach, applying Christian principles will resolve any issues one might have. If someone has a situation that might be weighing on them, such individuals believe going to church, praying, and reading the Bible should be sufficient for any situation one faces. If it goes beyond such levels, someone should go for Christian advice and instruction on following those principles and being more Christian. Such leaders object to the idea of therapeutic practice because in their minds, it introduces non-Christian ideas into a Christian's mind. Instead of seeing the process as productive for the believer, they see it as antithetical.

There is also a huge stigma against mental illness in many denominations. Older associations equate mental illness with demonic possession. Over and incorrect diagnoses and over-prescribing medications have not helped Christian leaders gain confidence in therapeutic process, causing suspicion of the overall process. While we know mental illness is not directly related to any sort of demonic possession, some out there still insist such is the case. They believe, once again, such issues can be resolved with enough prayer and faith, seeing therapy as delaying the process.

In Bible times, not every problem was solved by reading the Bible and living a Christian life. In fact, for much of Biblical history, people didn't have access to written copies of the Scriptures. There was no way to seek God except through process, whether that process was seeking counsel, meditation, prayer, or becoming aware of personal behaviors and their connections to one's life and history.

There is no contradiction between receiving wise counsel and faith. While yes, we need to find a counselor who guides through the process in the way we need, there is nothing wrong with having Jesus and a therapist if you feel that will work best for you. Sometimes we need longer-term help or more specified work for complex issues than a Christian minister or counselor can offer. Maybe we have an issue that requires deeper introspection and clarification. Whatever the reason, if you feel you need counseling – whether with your pastor, leader, or a trained therapist – there's nothing wrong with seeking sound methods to help you sort things out.

Older Women Dating Younger Men. What's Your Opinion?

When I was growing up, it was very rare to see a woman older than her husband or significant other. Such was often considered scandalous and improper. While no one ever said we shouldn't date younger men, it was something that wasn't ever discussed as an option.

Today it's not as uncommon to see partners of all genders in relationships with age gaps. Specifically answering your question, you do see older women with younger men more today than in years past. Some might even classify it as a trend, identifying women who prefer to date younger men as "cougars." It's obvious even though age gaps are becoming more common, older women dating younger men is still a subject of controversy. By the nickname alone it associates women with predatory behavior, as if they are staking out and seeking to ruin the lives of younger men. Is this an accurate portrayal of such relationships? What's more, does the Bible have to say about such relationships?

It should be said upfront that there are many different reasons why people pursue any relationship they might desire. There isn't one reason why someone might be attracted to or interested in someone younger or older, regardless of what stereotypes or common theories might say to the contrary. For every age and body type out there, there is someone who is attracted to it. This is just as true for younger men and older women as it is for anything else. Some men prefer older women; some women prefer younger men. While it might not be considered "the norm," it is no less a legitimate relationship than any other one that someone might choose to pursue.

Age gap relationships aren't new. If we look at the Bible, age differences were common in marriage relationships. As marriages were business transactions, age wasn't a consideration. While most examples involve older men and younger women (sometimes much younger women and much older men), there are instances where women were older in a relationship. Such would have been the case in levirate marriages, examples of which we can see below.

Judah got a wife for Er, his firstborn, and her name was Tamar. But Er, Judah's firstborn, was wicked in the LORD's sight; so the LORD put him to death.

Then Judah said to Onan, "Sleep with your brother's wife and fulfill your duty to her as a brother-in-law to raise up offspring for your brother." But Onan knew that the child would not be his; so whenever he slept with his brother's wife, he spilled his semen on the ground to keep from providing offspring for his brother. What he did was wicked in the LORD's sight; so the LORD put him to death also.

Judah then said to his daughter-in-law Tamar, "Live as a widow in your father's household until my son Shelah grows up." For he thought, "He may die too, just like his brothers." So Tamar went to live in her father's household. (Genesis 38:6-11)

That same day the Sadducees, who say there is no resurrection, came to him with a question. "Teacher," they said, "Moses told us that if a man dies without having children, his brother must marry the widow and raise up offspring for him. Now there were seven brothers among us. The first one married and died, and since he had no children, he left his wife to his brother. The same thing happened to the second and third brother, right on down to the seventh. Finally, the woman died. Now then, at the resurrection, whose wife will she be of the seven, since all of them were married to her?" (Matthew 22:23-28)

Levirate marriage was an ancient marriage custom found throughout the ancient world. Its purpose, as stated in Deuteronomy 25:5-6:

If brothers are living together and one of them dies without a son, his widow must not marry outside the family. Her husband's brother shall take her and marry her and fulfill the duty of a brother-in-law to her. The first son she bears shall carry on the name of the dead brother so that his name will not be blotted out from Israel.

In other words, levirate marriage was about family preservation. Families were patrilineal in nature and property passed between males. If a man died without a male heir, property couldn't pass to his wife or female children. The purpose, therefore, was to ensure property remained in families and the deceased were remembered through their lineage. First in line for levirate marriage was the closest male relative to the deceased (usually a brother). Levirate custom did extend beyond this sometimes, such as in the case of Ruth and Boaz, to nearest kin when there are no immediate male relatives.

What does this have to do with older women dating younger men? If a woman was married to one brother and then married another, there was always the possibility she was older than him (especially if the brother was younger than his deceased sibling). In the examples provided, we can see the women mentioned were older than their counterparts. Shelah, next in line in the levirate system, was so much younger than Tamar, he wasn't of marrying age! In the question of the woman with seven husbands, even if her first husband was older than her, running through each husband down to the youngest would mean she was older than some of the men at some point. In levirate systems fertility was paramount, so not only would a younger husband increase possible longevity of life, it would also increase chances of pregnancy.

I know that some desire Biblical evidence for everything; and in this instance, I have provided such in keeping with the question. I am also of the opinion not everything we do requires a Bible verse. As a woman who has dated men younger than myself, I can vouch there are great reasons to pursue a relationship with someone of a different age. Whether or not it's something you are comfortable pursuing is up to you as a person. Know, however, that if it's something you desire to do, there is nothing wrong with doing so.

Is Grief Different from Healing?

You've asked a complicated question that I will answer to the best of my ability. If I understand it properly, you are asking if grief is something that requires healing or if it is something different that does not. It's a complicated question because it is a both/and issue, not one that falls into the either/or category. If we see it through a broader view, it will help us understand the issue at hand.

Grief is a process. Whether or not one identifies it as a healing process is a matter of personal opinion. I do not see grief as a healing process, but rather as a massive life adjustment by which healing takes place. The "healing" of grief isn't so much about the death or loss involved, but about the resolution of many things connected to such that were part of someone's life for a very long time. For example, if someone's spouse dies, they are left with the huge adjustment of learning to re-live life without that person. They must sort through items, handle financial and estate matters, and notify people. The longer time goes by, the adjustment becomes more about personal loss rather than the person lost. There's the change to being single again, taking over household tasks that the other person once did, and feeling the emptiness that results. Whatever issues or situations were left undone are the survivors to face. It's a complex process that takes time, is not linear in its focus, and resurfaces periodically throughout life.

The reason I hesitate to define grief as something that requires healing is for this very reason. We associate healing with the idea that we "get over" something or move past something. Grief isn't that simple. It's something we learn to live with and hopefully, at some point in time, adjust enough to see the sun through to a better day. It's not something we "get over." We don't "recover" from grief. It's significant of a major life change that shifts one's focus and priorities in life. Dealing with it is a process, one that is very personal to each person that experiences it.

In grief, however, there is the opportunity for healing. Maybe it's not the grief itself we heal from, but things in our lives that require and press healing. It is in addressing some of these things that we are finally able to see our way to new life, even if it's not what we asked to have. The death of a relationship or situation offers the chance for rebirth, for new life. In death we find life. Whether it is birth into eternity or birthing something new this side of heaven, new life is always the ultimate result. Grief is the process of that new life: dying, waiting, and rising again to something else.

People who dwell in grief don't need long lectures, berating, positive affirmations, or gigantic pushes to do things. They need a listening ear, gentle consideration, and help to figure out what new life looks like for them. Patience is key. Love is essential. Being part of newness (even if you've been around awhile) brings positive change. Instead of worrying about how to define grief...just be there for someone as they go through the process.

OTHER BOOKS OF INTEREST

BY THE AUTHOR

Instruct the wise and they will be wiser still;
teach the righteous and they will add
to their learning.
The fear of the LORD is the beginning of wisdom,
and knowledge of the Holy One
is understanding.
For through wisdom your days will be many,
and years will be added to your life.

(Proverbs 9:9-11)

- *About My Father's Business: Professional Ministry for Kingdom Leaders* (Righteous Pen Publications, 2014)

- *Discovering Intimacy: A Journey Through the Song of Solomon* (Righteous Pen Publications, 2015)

- *The Divine Feminine: A Treatise on the Female in Christian Spirituality* (Photini Press, 2018)

- *The Fundamentals of Christian Counseling: In Theory and Practice* (Righteous Pen Publications, 2014)

- *A Heart God Can Use: The Journey to the Center of His Will* (Remnant Words, 2019)

- *Manifestations of the Spirit: The Work of the Holy Spirit in the Church and in Your Life* (Righteous Pen Publications, 2019)

- *Ministering to LGBTQ+ – And Those Who Love Them: A Primer for Queer Theology* (Apostolic Covenant Theological Seminary 2024)

- *Ministry School Boot Camp: Training for Helps Ministries, Appointments, and Beyond* (Righteous Pen Publications, 2014)

- *Ministry Officer Candidate School: Foundations for Christian Leadership* (Righteous Pen Publications, 2025)

- *Most Blessed Among All Women* (Photini Press, 2017)

- *Rubies and Pearls: One Hundred Days for Change* (Remnant Words, 2017)

- *Surrounded By So Great a Cloud of Witnesses: Women of Faith Who Revolutionized History* (Photini Press, 2018)

ABOUT THE AUTHOR

DR. LEE ANN B. MARINO

Once, on being asked by the Pharisees when
the Kingdom of God would come, Jesus replied,
"The coming of the Kingdom of God
is not something that can be observed,
nor will people say, 'Here it is,'
or 'There it is,' because the Kingdom of God
is in your midst."

(Luke 17:20-21)

Dr. Lee Ann B. Marino, Ph.D., D.Min., D.D. (she/her) is "everyone's favorite theologian" leading Gen X, Millennials, and Gen Z with expertise in leadership training, queer and feminist theology, general religion, and apostolic theology. She has served in ministry since 1998 and was ordained as a pastor in 2002 and an apostle in 2010. She founded what is now Sanctuary Apostolic Fellowship Empowerment (SAFE) Ministries in 2004. Under her ministry heading Dr. Marino is founder and Overseer of Sanctuary International Fellowship Tabernacle (SIFT) (the original home of National Coming Out Sunday) and The Sanctuary Network, and Chancellor of Apostolic Covenant Theological Seminary (ACTS).

Affectionately nicknamed "the Spitfire," Dr. Marino has spent over two decades as an "apostle, preacher, and teacher" (2 Timothy 1:11), exercising her personal mandate to become "all things to all people" (1 Corinthians 9:22). Her embrace of spiritual issues (both technical and intimate) has found its home among both seekers and believers, those who desire spiritual answers to today's issues.

Dr. Marino has preached throughout the United States, Puerto Rico, and Europe in hundreds of religious services and experiences throughout the years. A history maker in her own right, she has spent over two decades in advocacy, education, and work for and within minority spiritual communities (including African American, Hispanic, and LGBTQ+). She has also served as the first woman on all-male synods, councils, and panels, as well as the first preacher or speaker

273

welcomed of a different race, sexual orientation, or identity among diverse communities. Today, Dr. Marino's work extends to over 150 countries as she hosts the popular *Kingdom Now* podcast, which is in the top 20 percentile of all podcasts worldwide. She is also the author of over 35 books and the popular Patheos column, *Leadership on Fire*. To date, she has had five bestselling titles within their subject matter: *Understanding Demonology, Spiritual Warfare, Healing, and Deliverance: A Manual for the Christian Minister*; *Ministry School Boot Camp: Training for Helps Ministries, Appointments, and Beyond*; *Discovering Intimacy: A Journey Through the Song of Solomon*; *Fruit of the Vine: Study and Commentary on the Fruit of the Spirit*; and *Ministering to LGBTQ+ (and Those Who Love Them): A Primer for Queer Theology* (and its accompanying workbook).

As a public icon and social media influencer, Dr. Marino advocates healthy body image (curvy/full-figured), representation as a demisexual/aromantic, and albinism awareness as a model. Known to those she works with, she is a spiritual mom, teacher, leader, professor, confidant, and friend. She continues to transform, receiving new teaching, revelation, and insight in this thing we call "ministry." Through years of spiritual growth and maturity, Dr. Marino stands as herself, here to present what God has given to her for any who have an ear to hear.

For more information, visit her website at kingdompowernow.org.

9781940197562